POSITIVE PARENTING WITH A PLAN
(Grades K-12)

Matthew A. Johnson, Psy.D., MSW

with a foreword by Hillel I. Swiller, M.D.

FAMILY
Rules

PO Box 221974 Anchorage, Alaska 99522-1974

ISBN 1-888125-46-2

Library of Congress Catalog Card Number: 2002115983

Acknowledgments

THE WRITING OF ANY book is a major endeavor. A book cannot be written without encouragement, support, and assistance from many individuals. First, I thank my three children, Levi, Hannah, and Micah, who were loving and patient guinea pigs while I implemented FAMILY in our home. They are blessings from above as well as bona fide keepers.

I am indebted to my parents for their ongoing love and support throughout my life. Although we have had more than our fair share of dysfunctional times together, they always tried their best to teach me sound morals and values along with being confident with who I am and why I am on this planet. I am also indebted to L.D. and Darlene Mattson, along with their son, Scott, who have always been a second family to me. They taught me the importance of personal commitment to faith, hope, and love. The greatest of these is love.

I owe much to a few friends for their generosity, love, and ongoing encouragement they have extended to my family and me while helping us to reestablish our lives and my private practice in Grants Pass, Oregon. Also, I really appreciate the ongoing love and support from my dear friends, Andy and Brenda Ridgway.

I thank Janice Cocklereece for her transcription work which made writing this book much easier. I would much rather dictate than type. Many thanks to Jeni Taylor, Dr. David Jenkins, and Jeff Wheaton who provided their expertise while editing my rough draft. Their feedback was very direct but gentle and kind. I thank all the schools, churches, and civic groups who have sponsored FAMILY-Rules seminars. They have helped to spread the good news: "Every home needs a FAMILY."

Finally, I am particularly grateful to all of the families I have worked with in various treatment facilities, in my private practice, and via my FAMILY-Rules seminars. Their feedback in helping to tweak, tune, adjust, and modify the FAMILY-Rules system has been invaluable. Some of their stories are used as examples in this book to help further explain the philosophical underpinnings of the FAMILY-Rules system and the importance of implementing FAMILY in every home. Names, situations, and settings have been changed to protect confidentiality.

I had the Meanest Mother in the World

I HAD THE MEANEST mother in the world. While other kids had candy for breakfast, I had to eat cereal, eggs, and toast. While other kids had cake and candy for lunch, I had a sandwich. As you can guess, my dinner was different from other kids' dinners too. My mother insisted on knowing where we were at all times. She had to know who our friends were and what we were doing.

I was ashamed to admit it, but she actually had the nerve to break the child labor law. She made us work. We had to wash dishes, make the beds, and learn how to cook. That woman must have stayed awake nights thinking up things for us kids to do. And she insisted we tell the truth, the whole truth, and nothing but the truth.

By the time we became teenagers, she was much wiser and our life became more unbearable. None of this tooting the car horn for us to come running. She embarrassed us to no end by insisting that our friends come to the door to get us.

I forgot to mention that most of our friends were allowed to date at the mature age of 12 or 13, but our old fashioned mother refused to let us date until we were 15. She really raised a bunch of squares. None of us were ever arrested for shoplifting or busted for dope. And who do we have to thank for this? You're right, our mean mother.

I am trying to raise my children to stand a little straighter and taller and I am secretly tickled to pieces when my children call me mean. I thank God for giving me the meanest mother in the world. The world needs more mean mothers like mine.

Author Unknown

Foreword

AN ABSENCE OF STRUCTURE afflicts a vast number of contemporary American families. There are many sources of this dreadful phenomenon including substance abuse, mental illness, divorce, illegitimacy, financial pressures, and moral inadequacy, to name just a few. Whatever the primary sources of the lack of family structure may be, the absence of structure itself invariably leads the family further down the spiral of despair, dysfunction, disease and delinquency.

Dr. Matthew A. Johnson ("Dr. J.") and his FAMILY Rules parenting system offer a powerful alternative to family chaos. FAMILY Rules presents a solid and coherent structure for families in need. In this book, he first presents a philosophical and intellectual framework for FAMILY Rules and then presents the system itself in an absolutely clear and straightforward manner.

FAMILY Rules is a product of who and what "Dr. J." himself is, a child of a family with problems, an outstanding competitive athlete, a dedicated and highly trained professional, and a man of strong conviction who practices what he believes.

While FAMILY Rules is highly structured, it is not rigid. Within the structure is plenty of room for individuality and creativity just as the rules of basketball leave room for the individuality and creativity of a Michael Jordan or a Dr. J.

Families who understand and correctly and consistently implement FAMILY Rules will be protected from many of the most pernicious ills of our time. I am pleased to recommend FAMILY Rules.

Hillel I. Swiller, MD, FAPA, FAGPA
Clinical Professor of Psychiatry
Mount Sinai School of Medicine
New York, New York

Contents

Part 3   FAMILY Questions?

Part 4   Appendices

Introduction

I HAVE WRITTEN AND rewritten this book at least 100 times in my mind. I'm sure I'll rewrite it 100 more times in my mind after the first printing. *Positive Parenting with a Plan (Grades K-12): FAMILY-Rules*: referred to as FAMILY throughout the remainder of the book, is the summation of working for nearly two decades in the mental health field with children, adolescents, and parents. FAMILY is based on three basic principles: (1) More often than not, mothers are the primary caregivers and disciplinarians in the home. This parenting system honors that fact, (2) Kids need rules, and the FAMILY parenting system provides them, and (3) Discipline in the home is essential to a healthy home. FAMILY gives organization and structure for discipline, more than most other parenting systems available. It's also very simple to implement. Therefore, this specific parenting discipline system is the FAMILY of all parenting discipline systems. In summary, mothers rule, FAMILY has rules and FAMILY rules.

I have "begged, borrowed, and stolen" (only a figure of speech) the principles of FAMILY from my work in residential treatment facilities, group homes, inpatient treatment settings, and youth groups. I have taught FAMILY to over 4,000 families via my private practice and FAMILY seminars.

Before developing FAMILY, I was frustrated to see many young patients make tremendous progress through their work in various mental health settings, only to regress shortly after returning home. We as mental health professionals would work hard to stabilize a child's out of control behaviors via a consistently implemented behavior modification program. It never made any sense to me that both counselor

11

and patient put out so much effort, only to send the child back home to his or her parents, who were usually as dysfunctional as their child. In addition, these parents rarely had any consistent structure and organization in their home. Eventually the child would return to his or her inappropriate behaviors and the parents would call us up, yelling and complaining. One day it dawned on me. Why not teach parents the strategies that we as mental health professionals implement in group homes, residential treatment facilities, and acute care facilities for children? Parents could then continue the same process at home. As a result, FAMILY was conceived in my mind.

Since the conception of FAMILY, it has been <u>tweaked</u>, <u>tuned</u>, <u>adjusted</u>, and <u>modified</u> over time thanks to ongoing feedback from the parents and children who learned the system. There is, however, one consistent piece of feedback from parents I have been ignoring for many years: "You should write a FAMILY book and make it available nationwide so more families can benefit from the system." Also, many parents said to me, "You should teach FAMILY Rules seminars nationwide." Several parents told me they have tried other parenting approaches with far less success. Most parenting books and parenting seminars teach very important parenting principles as well as some useful tools for disciplinary interventions. However, they usually lack a complete system of organization and structure to assist parents with intervention tools for discipline in the home. FAMILY, on the other hand, is a complete system.

Over the years, I have used two excuses to ignore writing a book about FAMILY: (1) "I don't have the time to write a book because I'm overwhelmed by the time it takes to be a father, board member, coach, and psychologist in private practice;" and (2) "I don't have enough professional experience under my belt to present a credible and unique intervention strategy to assist parents and their children in their homes."

Well, much time has passed, and now I have no excuse. Don't worry, I'm still a husband and father. After teaching FAMILY to over 4,000 families with much success, and incorporating their feedback, I now believe I can offer a credible and unique behavior modification system to other families for use in their homes. I now feel compelled to write this book.

Part 1
Understanding
the Basics of FAMILY

1 Where's the Instruction Manual on Parenting?

"THEY DIDN'T GIVE US an instruction manual on parenting when we brought our child home from the hospital!" "They didn't give us a warranty either!" These are commonly stated phrases among parents I have worked with over the years. Most parents can relate to both statements. The "how to" questions of parenting never end. First, we have often wondered "where do the batteries go" in all three of my children? What about other "troubleshooting" problems such as when the talking, crying, screaming, fighting and laughing buttons get stuck in the "on" position? Where's the Prozac button so everyone is happy? Where's the Kaopectate button so the brown stuff firms up? Finally, where's the psychostimulant button so they can focus and slow down?

Second, there have been times when dads wanted to return the apparent defective product directly to the production plant; however, wives raised strong objections to this idea. It's one thing to watch the birth videos in reverse, it's another thing to ... well, you get the picture. So, I guess we all are kind of stuck with the little "Rug Rats," "Curtain Climbers," "Carpet Crawlers," "Teeny Boppers," "Crumb Crunchers," and "Adult Wannabe's." Besides, no other kids are as smart and as good looking as our children. Right? Right!

Problems arise around the age of two when our cute little toddlers start to say, "No." In our case, with Micah, it was "No. No. No. No." Okay, I confess, it is cute and sometimes funny at first. It is also developmentally necessary for our children to start the process of becoming their own individual selves—separate from mom and dad. However, as our toddlers pass through the "terrible-two's," become children, and inevitably teenagers, they say "no" louder and with much more frequency, determination, and defiance.

The challenge of parenting is to balance our children's developmental needs, such as autonomy, individuation, and identity with plain old common sense. We want them to take responsibility for their choices and to develop a healthy respect for authority. Therefore, the issues that parents want addressed in an "instruction manual for parenting" are the following: (1) help to better organize and structure their families, (2) practical parenting tools which will assist them in teaching the proper morals and values to their children, (3) assistance in clearly communicating expectations to their children while giving them reasonable rewards and consequences for their choices, and (4) an alternative to going insane or slowly torturing their kids to death. Just kidding! Please do not try this at home!

Let's face it, parents have a challenging task and they want to do it right the first time. Most parents desire to see their child grow up to become a successful contributing member of society rather than an inmate in the county jail or state correctional institution. Please take notice of the fact that I used the word "most" and not "all" when referring to parental desires for their children. Some parents don't appear to care at all as to how their children grow up. The truth is, parental action or inaction speaks louder than words.

We are living in troubled times when you consider how children and adolescents are behaving today. The terrible tragedy at Columbine High School in Littleton, Colorado confirms this harsh reality. This fact is true no matter where I travel in the United States or around the world. While in Western Samoa, I spoke with a parent from Australia and another parent from New Zealand who expressed their concerns about the poor choices adolescents are making in their countries as well as the disrespect they continually convey toward adult authority figures. After explaining FAMILY to them, they expressed an urgent desire to see FAMILY published and distributed in their countries, too. A look beneath the surface reveals that many parents are concerned, but don't know what to do. In most cases, parental action and/or inaction has contributed to their children's inappropriate behaviors.

Parental Action

Some examples of parental actions that contribute to a child's inappropriate, acting out behaviors are verbal, physical, and/or sexual abuse in the home, role-modeling poor attitudes about authority, poor diet, lack of exercise, and low self-esteem. Essentially, this is about parents not walking their talk or practicing what they preach. Quite frankly, consistency is a major challenge for all of us. From a personal perspective, it is an ongoing challenge for me to **Correctly** and **Consistently** implement FAMILY in my own home because I am a creature of habit just like everyone else (i.e., "the two 'C' words"). I like the comfort of daily routines even if those routines are self-serving, counter-productive to my goals for raising my children and counter productive to my own health. For me, the path of least resistance is the most comfortable path as well as the most nonproductive one. It took a public service reminder from a supportive friend to practice **Correct** and **Consistent** implementation of FAMILY in my own home—and I'm the author of the system! Imagine that! Consistent parenting helped my children to behave better.

I once worked with a family in Oregon. Martha, a very tall mother, took great pride in butting heads with school board members, teachers, and city officials. She talked openly in front of her children about the incompetence of various authorities. These authorities were always wrong and Martha was always right. Also, Martha always verbalized self-put downs concerning her height to her children. She viewed her height as a handicap and didn't wish this curse on anyone, especially her children.

Martha was shocked when I had the gall to suggest that possibly her parental role-modeling contributed to her very tall son's defiance toward the authority of school officials, as well as his low self-esteem concerning his own height. You see, Martha brought her son, Warren, into therapy because her son's defiance toward authority at school started to infiltrate her own home. Warren was telling her "no" more frequently and defiantly. What goes around comes around. She didn't like the idea that her actions contributed to her son's problem behaviors. I taught FAMILY to Martha and her husband which they reluctantly chose to implement in their home with their son. They were reluctant because they were required to walk the talk. Martha wasn't allowed to violate her own rules for her son. She couldn't talk negatively about authority figures, she couldn't swear, and she had to talk positively about her own height. Through counseling and the implementation of FAMILY in their home, the family was turned right side up. During the following year, I ran into Martha at the state fair. She shared with me that Warren was doing much better. He was no longer getting into trouble at school and he actually appreciated his height. She acknowledged her initial reluctance to implement FAMILY, but was glad she did. She was also glad I confronted her about low self-esteem issues concerning her own height which eventually effected her very tall son. The cognitive intervention strategies via counseling were also helpful in turning her thinking around in a more positive direction.

I could relate to Martha and her son, Warren, concerning their issues surrounding being very tall. I'm six feet nine inches tall and have been taller than my peers my whole life. While in grade school, I would often come home crying. Taking the time to uncover the reason, my mother discovered my peers were making fun of me because I was much taller than they were. They called me many names and excluded me from their games on the playground during recess. My mother is tall. She talked about her height and my own height with great pride. She taught me to think about my height in many positive ways. As a result, I have used my height to open doors for me socially, academically (via a college basketball scholarship), in the area of employment, and in the arena of public speaking. My height and humor go a long way when speaking to a group of people. Being a doctor of psychology helps as well. Finally, knowing and trusting in God is the icing on the cake that opens doors for success.

Another example of parental actions that contributed to their child's problems is in the case of Todd, Kris, and David. They were referred to my office in New Jersey because David was caught at school with marijuana, a marijuana pipe, and mushrooms. I was confused during the diagnostic interview as to why Todd and Kris, the parents, only verbalized concern about David's possession of mushrooms and not marijuana. After all, this was David's third offense involving the possession of marijuana. What parents in their right mind wouldn't be incensed by now?

I later put one and one together in the subsequent counseling sessions. Todd and Kris verbalized an ideology that society as a whole is wrong about narcotics and that all drugs should be legalized, especially marijuana. They openly espoused their ideology in front of David, and yet, they were surprised that he was busted for a third time on school grounds for possession of drugs. Duh! When I raised the possibility that their personal ideology was contributing to the delinquency of their minor, they genuinely looked puzzled. Although they thought the drug laws were wrong, they thought their son had enough common sense not to bring drugs to school. In their minds, the problem was their son's lack of common sense— not their ideology. They refused to learn FAMILY. Needless to say, in spite of all the wonderful counseling I had to offer, their son remains at high risk for using drugs and getting busted again for possession on school grounds. When the inevitable happens, I'm sure they'll blame their son's lack of common sense or my counseling—not their ideology nor their own parental actions. After all, they're right and it's the rest of us who are wrong.

Parental Inaction

Some examples of parental inaction that contribute to childhood problems and defiance consist of neglect, abandonment, absences due to a workaholic attitude and/or the lack of taking disciplinary action. Parents are often afraid to act, fearing that their child may run away, become violent, withdraw, never talk to them again, or commit an act of self-harm, including the possibility of suicide.

I once worked with a single parent named, Connie, who had an adolescent son, Ed, and an adolescent daughter, Teresa. Ed and Teresa slapped, punched, kicked, and cussed at their mother with a sailor's vocabulary. They often slammed her against the wall and threatened her life. Connie experienced constant verbal and physical abuse by Ed and Teresa when they were home. They came and went as they pleased and defied school authority as well. Connie feared putting her foot down with her children because she didn't want to be physically abused more frequently than she already was. They also threatened her with the possibility that they would leave and go live with their father in another state if she didn't let them do what they wanted to do.

I helped Connie to rebuild her self-esteem after several counseling sessions. She needed to see herself as having a parental backbone of steel rather than a wet spaghetti noodle. Then I taught her FAMILY and helped explain it to her children. I never heard so much swearing in my life and I used to play college basketball (my teammates were not missionaries in the locker room). Connie put her foot down in one session and told Ed and Teresa that they were going to follow FAMILY in their home or they could go live with their father. Connie also told them that she would press assault charges if they ever physically abused her again. Connie took the wind out of Ed and Teresa's sails as they never really wanted to go live with their father. They were merely using the threat of leaving their mother as a means of control over her. Once I convinced Connie that Ed and Theresa were bluffing her like a hustler in a Las Vegas poker game, she called their bluff. They were no longer king of the hill and went tumbling down the hill while their mother ascended to the throne. Their family was turned right side up. As a result, their behaviors improved greatly at home and at school.

Approximately two years later, Connie returned to my office at her children's insistence. They all informed me that their family life was taking a turn for the worse again. Ed and Theresa were not happy campers. Apparently, Connie was dropping the ball concerning correct and consistent implementation of FAMILY in their home. Remember "the two 'C' words?" Correct and consistent implementation. Surprisingly, Ed and Teresa were demanding the reinstitution of FAMILY in their home. They were tired of their mother's yelling and inconsistent implementation of rewards and consequences. It takes a great amount of effort to maintain a consistent bedtime when the sun is still high up in the sky at midnight. Connie fell victim to the Alaska summer - the land of the midnight sun. It was easier to let her kids run free than correctly and consistently implement FAMILY.

Connie also disregarded the doctor's orders, or in this case, the psychologist's orders. Whenever I teach FAMILY to families, I tell them to take FAMILY until it is all gone. Usually, the family members will look at me with weird expressions on their faces and ask, "What do you mean by 'until it's all gone?'" At that point, I provide a little education utilizing an analogy about physicians instructing their patients to take their medication as prescribed until it's all gone. Often, physicians warn their patients about discontinuing their medication simply because they are starting to feel better. Some people will save the remainder of their medication so they will have it available the next time they are sick because they don't want to have to endure the inconvenience and expense of seeing their physician again. However, because they choose not to listen to their physician, and finish their medication, the illness comes back and hits them with a double strength whammy. These patients end up going back to their physician, eventually spending more time and money getting over their sickness. They would have gotten better sooner if had they just followed their physician's orders.

In the same manner, families need to take FAMILY until it's all gone. In other words, FAMILY should be implemented in the home until the last child has turned eighteen, graduated from high school, and has moved out. Connie's parental inaction led to her own chastisement by her son and daughter, who used to verbally and physically abuse her. Connie thought their home life was going much better so she backed off of the correct and consistent implementation of FAMILY in their home. Ed and Teresa wanted consistent structure and order in their home and turned their mom in to the FAMILY police. That would be me or any other FAMILY Rules counselor. (See Appendix A for more information.)

Finally, parental inaction can be clearly seen in the case of Jason and Cathy concerning their adopted son, Carl. For many years, Carl seemed like the perfect kid; however, he slowly began to change for the worse as his adoption issues began to surface. He began to hang out with the wrong crowd, smoke, and use drugs. Eventually, he dropped out of school. He threatened to beat up his mother and father whenever they attempted to confront him about his problems. They were legitimately afraid to take action because Carl had beaten up his older brother, Keith, with a baseball bat during the previous year. Their parental paralysis, caused by fear of Carl's threats, was contributing to his demise.

Jason and Cathy are humble, gracious, God-loving people. They decided to give Carl space and love him back into being a good boy, but his problems worsened. Unknowingly, they were loving him to death. They sought out my counseling and psychological testing services to help them deal with Carl. After meeting with Carl and his parents for a couple of sessions, I had to inform Jason and Cathy that Carl was in need of long-term residential treatment to address his conduct disorder. Carl's attitudes and behaviors were greatly out of control. He had no respect for his parents, other authority figures, or for himself. He was headed down the proverbial slippery slide to incarceration or a premature death. He needed intensive long-term residential treatment immediately or it would be, "Hasta-la-bye-bye" for him one way or another.

Needless to say, my recommendation was a real challenge for Jason and Cathy to accept. They did not want to send Carl away again. They had already sent him to a snow board school in the lower 48 states and saw no improvements. Also, because Jason and Cathy sent him away for treatment, Carl claimed abandonment issues related to his adoption. Carl knew how to push their guilt buttons. I assured them that the World Wide Association of Specialty Programs (www.wwasp.com) have high quality treatment facilities, have a fantastic success rate, and most likely have the best programs on Planet Earth to help their son. I gave them names and phone numbers of other parents who had sent their children to this program so they could talk with them for encouragement. I also told them about a support group for parents with troubled teens that meets at the local hospital in Fairbanks every other Sunday. Jason and Cathy understandably hesitated. They needed time to think and pray.

As time progressed, Carl's behaviors worsened. He made it clear that he was his own boss and was not going to obey his parents or any other adult authority figures. The occasional resurfacing of Carl's nice qualities kept his parents hanging on to a thin thread of hope that he would ultimately change and they would not need to intervene. The sun went down on their hope and Jason and Cathy eventually realized and accepted the fact that Carl needed residential treatment as soon as possible. He was almost seventeen so they only had one year left to effect positive change in his life. They were finally willing to put their foot down and implement the "teeth" FAMILY provides and encourages as a last resort option. Thus, I provided Carl's parents with professional escort options and ended up escorting him to Western Samoa. I'll provide more details on Carl's story later in the book. Stay tuned.

Children Have Free Will

Although parental actions or inactions speak louder than words and greatly influence the family, please don't forget that children and adolescents also have free will. They can choose to obey or disobey in spite of parental influences to the contrary.

I have worked with almost perfect parents who appeared to have a D.C. sniper or international terrorist for a child. They walk the talk, love their children unconditionally, provide them with correct and consistent structure, and their children still choose to jump off into the deep end of the cesspool of defiance and disobedience. Also, I have worked with "parents from hell," who have children on the honor roll, participating in school sports and clubs, and don't drink, smoke, or chew and they don't hang out with kids who do.

While attending graduate school in Oregon, I worked with a gentleman named Allen. He was a nice man who was overwhelmed by much pain and anger rooted in his past. Allen grew up in a home with parents who loved him very much. They poured their time and resources into correcting his developmental problems (e.g., feet, hearing, speech, and orthodontic problems) and they invested themselves into his athletic development. This investment eventually led to his obtaining a full-ride scholarship to play collegiate football. However, in spite of their love and devotion, they also had problems in their family. Allen's mom's alcoholism kicked in right around the time he entered the ninth grade. His father always had an anger management problem and the stress of his job didn't help matters. Allen's parents would occasionally take turns verbally and physically abusing their kids - his mom, during her drunken states, and his dad, during his anger episodes.

Once, when Allen was a senior in high school, his mom came into his bedroom in the early morning hours. Allen was sound asleep.

His mom was drunk. She proceeded to slap Allen out of his sleep and told him what a lousy son he was. Her tirade went on for a few minutes while Allen laid there in shock. He was very confused by her words because he was receiving very good grades, active in sports, participating in the school choir, active in the youth group at church, and he never drank alcohol or used drugs. Allen's mom ended her tirade by stating, "I wish you were never born!" She left his room. Allen laid in his bed, crying, staring up at his ceiling in the darkness. Although he loved his parents, Allen was hurt and angry at God for sticking him in this family. He prayed, "What did I ever do to deserve this treatment, God?"

For as long as Allen could remember, his parents seldom ever got along. He remembered being a very frightened three-year-old, lying in his upstairs bedroom, while his parents were downstairs yelling and screaming at each other. This went on just about every night. In spite of this, Allen sometimes felt safe because he was in his bed, in his room, with his blanket. Now, fifteen years later, their anger had finally invaded the refuge of Allen's bedroom. Allen's mom returned to his bedroom five minutes later crying, still very drunk, wanting to apologize for what she had said. She wanted Allen to forgive her and she wasn't going to leave his bedroom until he gave her a hug and a kiss. Needless to say, Allen did not want to touch her. Her breath smelled like a brewery. If someone lit a match at that moment in time, they probably would have lost the backside of their house. Allen was hurt, angry, and wanted to vomit due to the stench. The thought of her hugging and kissing him was more than he could handle.

At that time in Allen's life, during his senior year, he was quite large for his age. Being a rather big football player, he could have picked up his mom and thrown her out of his room; however, Allen loved her and respected her. Allen chose to honor her with his behaviors rather than to use her alcoholism and verbal and physical abuse as an excuse to hurt her back. Allen eventually gave his mom a hug and a kiss just to get her out of his bedroom. She left his room feeling better. Allen still laid in his bed, crying, staring up at the ceiling, asking God, "Why?!!" The next morning, Allen's mom acted like nothing happened the night before. He was very hurt. Years later, Allen learned that his mom was experiencing an alcoholic blackout. She had damaged brain cells from her drinking. Alcohol had damaged her brain cells so much she could not remember what happened that night in Allen's bedroom.

In spite of the occasionally abusive environment that Allen grew up in as a child and adolescent, he still knew the difference between right and wrong and he chose to do what was right. Allen did not use his parents' shortcomings and mistakes as an excuse to behave in the same inappropriate ways. Thanks to the positive influence of Allen's youth pastor, his goal as an adolescent was to honor his dad and mom no matter what. Allen never got drunk, high, nor did he ever assault anyone. Yet, it is amazing to me how many times I encounter adolescents in my private practice who use their dysfunctional family environments as an excuse to behave like Mike Tyson or Marv Albert. They are constantly 'biting' the hands that feed them. Although parents can influence their children for better or worse, never forget that a child's "free will" is always an important variable that is mixed into the stew pot of life. A child can choose to behave right even though raised wrong. Another child can choose to behave wrong even though raised right. This can be very perplexing at times. Nevertheless, children should be held accountable for their choices. Sometimes parents opt not to hold their children accountable because of their own guilt from past parental mistakes. This parental inaction only leads to the creation of monsters in their home.

As I was previously saying, children have free will. FAMILY is not a "let's blame the parents" book. Rather, it's a "let's help the parents increase the odds of raising emotionally healthy and obedient children" book. Perfect children is not the goal of FAMILY. Increased compliance with and respect for adult authority is the goal of FAMILY via positive parenting. "Honor your father and mother" is not a bad virtue for children to learn. Most parents would not argue with this goal, but surprisingly, some parents do. Imagine that. I will comment in more detail concerning this sad truth in the next chapter.

2 *The Philosophical Underpinnings of FAMILY*

ALL EXISTING SYSTEMS of parenting have philosophical underpinnings as their foundation. This is the driving force behind what makes any parenting system work, if it works. Likewise, FAMILY has philosophical underpinnings that make the parenting discipline system work in the home. Many parents lack any kind of a parenting philosophy in their home other than relying on thoughts and feelings once experienced in childhood: "When I'm a parent, I'm not going to raise my kids the way my parents raised me!" Unlike some other parenting systems, FAMILY provides you with more than just philosophical underpinnings for raising your children in the real world. Instead, FAMILY also provides parents with specific steps to implement the philosophy while still allowing parents the opportunity to incorporate their own unique values and morals. The remainder of this chapter will identify and explain the philosophical underpinnings of FAMILY.

1. The "real world" is ordered and structured and the lack of order and structure results in chaos.

You will find some form of order and structure most everywhere you go on the earth. These important variables make the world turn. Without order and structure, we wouldn't know where to go or what to do next. How would we prioritize our goals without knowing the objectives and mission statement? How are decisions to be made? We all can't be the head. Someone has to be the arms, hands, legs, and feet. Someone has to clean the mess at the bottom and take out the trash. All positions are equally important in making order and structure work. Whether we are talking about various international organizations such as the United Nations, NATO or OPEC; or national governments such as the United States, Russia, or China; or State governments such as New York, Texas, or California; or local governments such as the city assembly, mayor's office, or the school board; or grass roots groups such as MADD, Guardian Angels, or NAACP; or private groups such as churches, synagogues, the Rotary Club, or Boy Scouts, organization and structure are the bones that hold everything together. Without order and structure, we would all be like lost sheep without a shepherd. We would all be wandering around in the wilderness without purpose or direction. As a result, chaos would ensue like in Cambodia, Somalia, Bosnia, Kosovo, East Timor, or Tallahassee, Florida. Just kidding, Florida!

Can you imagine being lucky enough to win two front row tickets on the fifty yard line to watch the Super Bowl? The top two NFL teams are playing for the championship. You arrive at the stadium with your child and there are no lines, just masses of people swarming around the entire building trying to get inside. You see people pushing and shoving while others are yelling obscenities at the gatekeepers. It takes several hours just to get inside. You are a little troubled by the lack of organization at the gates, but you'll manage, because you are at the Super Bowl for free and you have the best seats in the house! You walk down toward your seats and stop in your tracks as you observe two individuals attempting to obtain their seats next to yours. There is an intoxicated mob of strong men, World Wrestling Federation material, with painted faces that grab the two individuals and throw them over the railing to the ground below. You contact the stadium security to inform them about what you just witnessed as well as your desire to obtain your prized seats. The stadium chief security officer laughs at you. He says, "It's first come first served, Mac! Go find some empty seats!" Suddenly, you realize that you won't be watching the game from the best two seats in the stadium.

You're finally seated in the last two open seats at the top of the stadium behind one of the goal post, when the coin toss occurs. The captains of the team calling the coin toss didn't guess right and decide to beat up the officials. The sidelines clear and a brawl occurs. It takes an hour to get both teams back to their sidelines, and the injured off the field. While waiting, you talk with the one-eyed guy in the seat next to yours. You know, the guy with a patch over his eye and a scar across the front of his neck. After some discussion, you learn that he acquired his ticket for this game from an old lady he beat up outside the stadium. He also explains how he lost his eye and got the scar at the last two Super Bowls.

The team finally kicks off and the other team receives the ball. You notice that there are no officials on the field and the clock is not running. The players are throwing the ball back and forth and running anywhere they want to, on and off the field. No one is listening to their coach. After ten more minutes of observation, you quietly exit the stadium because you and your child want to leave alive and unharmed. You have had enough of chaos. Organization and structure would have made your Super Bowl experience much more enjoyable. Fortunately for football fans, the Super Bowl is run with a high degree of professionalism, organization and structure. Most of us have noticed this fact over the years from the best seats in the house - on the couch at home, strategically located near the kitchen and bathroom. These seats are cheap and we won't miss the Super Bowl commercials.

2. A hierarchy of authority and a healthy respect for it is a vital part of making order and structure work effectively.

Once again, everywhere you go on the earth, you will find evidence of the necessity of order and structure. As previously stated, someone has to be the head. Too many chefs in the kitchen can ruin a good meal. Every church has a pastor or priest. Every synagogue has a rabbi. Every school has a principal. Every city has a mayor. Every state has a governor. Every country has a prime minister, king, president or dictator. A healthy respect for those in authority is definitely a vital part of making order and structure work effectively.

Now imagine your child attending a middle school or high school where the students lack a healthy respect for and compliance to their teachers' and principal's authority. The students attend class when they want, fight in the hallways, bring weapons to school, buy and sell drugs on campus, curse at the teachers, and dress offensively without much, if any, consideration for the consequences. Imagine that you want your child to learn in a safe, organized and structured environment, but the school authorities fear implementing consequences. They fear being sued by litigious, irresponsible parents who are more interested in gaining a quick dollar than they are in having their children learn anything at all, especially respect and responsibility. You also learn that the school authorities fear taking a stance because their own school board may not back them up due to the very same fear of possible litigation. As a result, imagine yourself placing your child in a private school or charter school setting where the tolerance level for inappropriate behaviors is much lower and the teachers are supported by their administrators and parents. A civil suit is the last thing on their mind. Teaching children "the three R's" is the primary focus. Finally, everyone knows that the child will receive consequences at school and at home for breaking the rules, especially for being disrespectful toward authority figures. Imagine that! Parents, teachers and administrators working together, clearly communicating, can foster a healthy respect for authority in the students at home, school and the community.

Please do not mistake the above paragraph as an endorsement of private or charter schools over public schools. I bee edukated en dee publik skoolz. I am very happy with the public education I received at Morningside Elementary School, Leslie Middle School, and South Salem High School in Salem, Oregon. I'm pleased with the public education I received at the University of Alaska at Anchorage as well as at Rutgers University in New Jersey. Finally, I'm pleased with the private education I received at George Fox University in Newberg, Oregon. My oldest son has attended both private and public schools. I have been pleased with both learning environments. At present, all three children attend public schools in Grants Pass, Oregon. There are pro's and con's to both settings. Nevertheless, regardless of the setting, if students lack a healthy respect for authority at school, none of us as parents will be pleased with the learning environment. Most parents would perceive such a disorderly school setting as being poorly structured and ineffective in addressing our children's educational needs. We can all work together to improve our children's respect for the authority, organization, and structure in both public and private educational settings.

3. Authority flows downward; however, without checks, balances, and feedback there is a increased risk of developing a dictatorship (i.e., Absolute power corrupts - ask Adolph Hitler).

The vice-president doesn't tell the president what to do. The employee doesn't tell the employer what to do. The defendant doesn't tell the judge what to do. Finally, a child does not tell a parent what to do. It is a well known fact around the world that authority flows downward. Just ask the dissidents at Tienaman Square in China. I support what they were trying to do the day they were murdered by their own military. I'll take democracy over communism any day of the week. Nevertheless, the dissidents knew they were taking a major life-threatening risk by defying the authority of their nation. Our own forefathers knew the risk as well when they defied the King of England and his Redcoats. The Confederates knew the risk when they took on President Lincoln and the Yankee soldiers. There is power behind authority. Right or wrong, it is this power that makes authority effective. However, absolute power corrupts. It is important for people in positions of authority to be open to feedback from those lower on the totem pole of hierarchy. Otherwise, they too will become an absolute dictatorship and develop major blind spots to the error of their ways.

Adolph Hitler was destined for leadership. Initially, he wanted to study in seminary and become a man of the cloth. He had a strong desire to lead others down, what he perceived to be, a righteous path. Unfortunately, instead of seminary, the doors for the military, and eventually politics, opened up. He was not open to feedback from those serving directly underneath him. His absolute power, his self-perceived righteousness, and his unwillingness to listen to those serving below him eventually corrupted his own heart and mind in addition to the many Germans who blindly followed him. As a result, some of Hitler's own men tried to assassinate him without success. He was bound and determined to demonstrate the dominance of a white Aryan nation. Fortunately, Jessie Owens, an African-American, rained on Hitler's racist parade during the Olympics in Munich, Germany. Jessie Owens outran Hitler's best athletes and took the gold medal back to the United States. Unfortunately, Hitler's leadership abilities were used to murder millions of men, women, and children. You know how the story ends. The Americans and Russians closed in on Berlin and Hitler's defeat was imminent. He ended up murdering his wife and killing himself. Absolute power corrupts and leads to very disappointing conclusions that affect many lives.

Imagine a parent who becomes an absolute dictator in the home. The parental dictator believes he or she knows what is best for the family. The spouse and children are out to lunch. The spouse greatly desires to co-parent, making decisions together, but is forbidden the opportunity to do so because of a lack of cooperation, apathy, insults, abuse, or threats of divorce often used by partental dictators. Imagine the children becoming angry, depressed, and possibly dabbling in inappropriate activities as an act of rebellion against the dominant tyrant in the home. Imagine the spouse of the dictator retreating into his or her own world in order to cope with the harsh reality of living behind the iron curtain where fear of being shot discourages scaling the wall to escape. This is not an environment that anyone would want to live in whether it is a communist country or an extremely dysfunctional family. Finally, imagine watching another movie on TV about some kid that shoots his father because of a history of physical abuse toward himself and his mother. How about a TV show depicting an abused woman who sets her husband's bed on fire as a desperate act to escape. Unfortunately these events have happened and, as previously mentioned, absolute power corrupts and leads to very disappointing conclusions. There is a better way. Keep on reading.

4. Families need to be ordered, structured and have a hierarchy of authority. Authority flows downward within families - not upward (i.e., Children must learn to respect authority - parents, teachers, police, clergy, etc.).

Without repeating the obvious, I will assume that you have thoroughly read the proceeding philosophical underpinnings. I was taught in some of my social work and psychology classes that the ideal family system is a democratic one. Everyone has an equal say and equal vote. The philosophy of democratic parenting was also promoted in some treatment environments where I worked. I was young and idealistic when I first entered the mental health profession. My instructors certainly knew better than what my parents demonstrated for me while I was growing up. Therefore, I attempted to help families learn and practice the democratic model of parenting. There was only one problem. It never worked. Parents quickly became frustrated because common sense told them that they should have authority and power in the home, but these so called educated clinicians, including myself, were telling them to parent differently. I remember parents yelling at me about how their kids were going to get away with murder if they actually practiced this model of democratic parenting. I would look at them with a patronizing smile and gently encourage them to defy common sense and practice democratic parenting. Again, it never worked. At this time, I would like to extend a thousand apologies to those families, as should any clinician that promotes the democratic model of parenting. Elevating clinical ideology over the practical realities of life and good behavioral science is self-serving and morally reprehensible.

Fortunately, I was exposed to working in other therapeutic treatment environments where democratic parenting was not practiced. Instead, parents were encouraged to take control of their home by becoming benevolent dictators. In other words, parents were encouraged to lovingly assert their authority and seek compliance from their children concerning their parental values and morals. Although parents were directed to listen to their child's thoughts and feelings concerning various issues with a sensitive ear, ultimately, the parents had the final say. There were only two votes – dad's and mom's. Children were taught that their parents were in charge and they needed to learn how to submit to their parents' authority, as well as submitting to the authority of other adults at school, church, synagogue, and in the community. I began to see the benefits of behavior modification and how it's techniques were used successfully to gain compliance from children toward parents and other authority figures.

Eventually, I began to "beg, borrow, and steal" various concepts of behavior modification from my experiences working in different therapeutic settings and from behavioral research. As a result, FAMILY was born. Occasionally, I'll have parents in my office who want help getting their adolescent's attitudes and behaviors under control, but they want me to teach them the model of democratic parenting. I flat out refuse to teach them this model and offer FAMILY as a successful alternative. Sometimes I have to refer these parents to another counselor, but most will reluctantly try to learn and implement FAMILY in their home. Some parents have heard success stories from their friends about FAMILY and become eagerly willing to try it in their own home. Sometimes, I'll receive a letter or a phone call from these reluctant parents extending appreciation for my sticking to my guns and refusing to teach them democratic parenting. They often share many examples of positive changes in their family due to the correct and consistent implementation of FAMILY (i.e., "the two 'C' words").

5. A parent's primary responsibility is to prepare their child(ren) for the "real world" which is ordered, structured and requires a healthy respect for authority.

If the real world is ordered, structured and requires a healthy respect for authority, then why on earth would parents want to teach their children that these realities don't matter? These kinds of parents are doing their children and the community a great disservice. They are setting their children up for a lifetime of hardship and failure. Parents must take the time, and it does take time, to teach their children correctly and consistently that the real world has rules, regulations, laws, policies, and procedures. These rules need to be obeyed because breaking them can result in unemployment, prison, divorce, or death. Parents are doing their children and community a great service when they teach their children a healthy respect for authority. This is adequate preparation for the real world.

Unfortunately, some adults are unwilling to change their own habits or take the necessary time to correctly and consistently discipline their children. I have worked with some parents who fear taking the reigns of control away from their children because of possible resulting tension, conflict, and rebellion. I try to help them understand that they should fear what will happen to their children if they don't put their foot down now. Their child may wind up strung out on drugs, living on the streets, selling their bodies, incarcerated in a youth facility, or dead. Fear of the unknown can be paralyzing for many parents.

Speaking of fear, a healthy respect for authority requires reverent fear. Some therapists, especially those utilizing the democratic model of parenting, will argue against parents utilizing reverent fear as one of their parenting intervention strategies. However, fear is not always a bad thing. Reverent fear is good. There is an Old Testament verse that goes something like this, "The fear of God is the beginning of wisdom." I believe this verse conveys the truth that only a moron would tell God and his commandments to take a hike. On the other hand, those who are wise will listen to and obey God. They fear God's consequences if they don't obey. There is a verse in the New Testament that goes something like this, "Perfect love casts out fear." I believe this verse conveys the truth that eventually an individual will want to listen to and obey God. Over time, he or she eventually realizes that God's commandments were given as an act of love. His commands protect us from harm rather than act as a list of divine rules to ruin our day. In the same way, children who are correctly and consistently disciplined by their parents eventually realize that their parents' discipline is an act of love - not an attempt to ruin their children's lives.

An example of reverent fear being good would be teaching your toddlers not to run around in the parking lot at the grocery store. If they do, they might have an appointment with "Mr. Spanky" or worse, become a parking lot pancake. Another example would involve teaching your adolescent children that they are not going to curse at their teachers or go to parties and get drunk or high. If they do, they will endure consequences at home they will live to regret. These consequences do not involve physical abuse and/or prolonged torture. Children who respect and reverently fear authority at home will respect and reverently fear authority away from home.

The bottom line is, regardless of what some mental health professionals think, fear is a part of life and helps to make the world go round. Without fear, we would be in a heap of trouble. Years ago, when a friend and I were walking along a path on the Russian River in Alaska, we rounded a corner and ran right into a grizzly bear. The bear was only five feet away from us. The grizzly bear's face looked shocked and I'm pretty sure our faces looked the same too. I guarantee it! The grizzly bear turned around and ran about 50 feet and so did we in the opposite direction. Then the bear stood on it's hind legs to look over the brush to see what we were doing. We waved our hands high up in the air and yelled and screamed. We were hoping to scare the bear away. Unfortunately, this grizzly bear had an attitude problem. He growled, dropped down on all four legs, and charged right at us. We were armed only with our fishing poles.

My friend started to run and I grabbed his shoulder and told him, "Walk fast but don't run! You'll kick in his instincts to chase!" I followed my friend, maintaining a brisk pace, while the grizzly bear followed behind me down the path. Fear is good! Every time I looked over my shoulder to see if the grizzly bear was still behind us, he would growl and charge at me. I prayed like I never prayed before. Fear is good! We continued our brisk pace back to the trailhead that originally brought us down to the river. I looked over my shoulder again. The grizzly bear growled and charged again. I prayed. Fear is good! Finally, we reached the bottom of the hill. The grizzly bear was gone. Now, I was really scared. Where was the bear now? Fear is really good! We ran up the hill to my truck and climbed in back of it. Our hearts were pounding and we both were thanking God that we went to the bathroom before we walked down that trail to the Russian River.

Two days later, I read in the *Anchorage Daily News* that the Fish and Game officers had to shoot the same grizzly bear because he was charging other fishermen. The grizzly bear was trying to intimidate the fishermen in order to get them to drop their fish. He wanted an easy free meal. Unfortunately for the grizzly bear, he lost his fear of man. He was starting to physically bump into them to increase his intimidation. Therefore, he had to be shot. Fear is good! Fear makes the world go round. If we lose our fear, we get into big trouble. Parents need to teach this reality to their children. Today, many children and adolescents lack reverent fear of parents, teachers, police, clergy, and God.

6. Written rules help to clarify expectations which ultimately increases compliance and decreases inappropriate behaviors for most individuals.

Let's face it. Everywhere we go on the planet, rules, laws, regulations, treaties, policies and procedures are written down. They help us know how to behave with one another. Written rules act as a legal, ethical, and/or social contract between individuals, institutions, and governments. If these written standards are not complied with, then people lose their jobs, go to prison, pay penalties and interest, or work off community service hours. Nations might even go to war if a treaty is broken. The rules are written down at schools, churches, synagogues, work, clubs, governments, bars, and even on airplanes.

Every institution on the planet has taken the time to develop and post written rules except the most important institution in the world - the family. In the family, most parents have the rules listed in their minds only. Mom has a list of rules floating around inside her head and dad has a list of rules floating around inside his head. Some of these rules overlap in agreement; however, mom has rules that dad doesn't know about, or he does know about them and doesn't like them. Likewise, dad has a list of rules in his head that mom doesn't know about, or she does know about them and she doesn't like them either. This common scenario in most homes leads to great tension and conflict between spouses as well as between parents and their children.

The fact that most parents don't write down their rules for the family often causes their children to conduct Vulcan mind-melds to obtain the rules from their parents' brains. In other words, many children have to guess at what will or won't please their parents each day. Whether or not certain rules will be enforced may depend on one or both parents mood and energy levels. How confusing for the kids! Parents are supposed to prepare their children for living in the real world. Doesn't it make sense that the rules at home should be written down just like everywhere else on the planet? Who can argue against plain old common sense? Oops! I spoke too soon.

I once talked with a therapist who I will refer to as Clyde. He did not see the value in writing down the rules in the home. Clyde wanted to see the research to back up my philosophical statement: "Written rules help to clarify expectations which ultimately increases compliance and decreases inappropriate behaviors for most individuals." Well, first things first. I informed Clyde that a former psychology instructor of mine once stated during a statistics lecture, "Good research often confirms common sense to be true" or "What everyone pretty much already knew to be true is actually true." Secondly, I reminded Clyde that everywhere we go on the planet, important rules, laws, regulations, treaties, policies and procedures are written down. It is a way of life for all institutions, micro and macro, to help clarify expectations via appropriate communication. In other words, written rules help us to stay on the same page (pun intended).

Finally, I informed the skeptical therapist, Clyde, that if writing down the rules was good enough for the State Division of Occupational Licensing (SDOL) as well as God, then it was good enough for me. Clyde responded, "What do you mean by that?" I responded, "If the SDOL thought it was important enough to specifically spell out in a handbook what it takes to obtain or lose a license to work in the mental health field, then it is good enough for me. Also, if God thought it was important enough to have the Old and New Testaments recorded, including the Ten Commandments, in order to clarify His expectations for the human race and to increase our compliance with His standards, then it is good enough for me today. I'll use the same method with my children in our home."

I explored further why Clyde was being so apprehensive about something that made absolute common sense. He shared about his personal preference to "fly by the seat of my pants" without having to adhere to much order and structure. Clyde wasn't use to imposed boundaries and accountability and often, unknowingly, violated the boundaries of others. When boundaries were clarified for Clyde, he would become angry and oppositional. I wonder why Clyde was skeptical? Perhaps some unresolved issues were interfering there, huh? Clyde didn't want to be confused by the reality of common sense. The scary thing is that there are therapists like Clyde out there who unknowingly mess up your kids. I meant "work" with your kids.

Before I explain how the parenting system works to children and adolescents, I often share the following analogy with them in my private practice or at my FAMILY seminars. I ask them to imagine how they would think and feel if they woke up the next morning and read in the newspaper, watched on TV or heard on the radio that the governor of their state had stepped down from office. In addition, the state legislature had suspended itself and all state law. There were no more local or state police, the military bases were closed, and everyone was released from jail and prison. Most kids look shocked and tell me that they would feel very afraid of what others might do to them and their families. Naturally, there are always a few oppositional kids that say something like, "Cool!" I always respond by saying, "Cool, huh? So it would be cool if Joe Schmoe comes by your house, blows your dad away, slices your mothers throat, rapes and tortures you before burning you alive in your home, after, of course, looting your home for all the money and valuables they can find?"

Even the most oppositional children are eventually willing to concede that written rules help to protect all of us from others as well as ourselves. Defiant children are used to living by a double standard and they don't like having it pointed out to them. They like to have everyone follow the rules, but they don't want to live under the same obligation. Oppositional children want their parents to care for them by providing food, clothing, shelter, education, and medical attention. However, they also want to come and go as they please, drink and take drugs, smoke, skip school, cheat, steal, have sex, and have the right to treat others rudely. They want to be masters of their own destiny and live by their own set of rules, even if their rules violate the rules in their home, school, church, synagogue, and/or community. Basically, they want their cake and the freedom to eat it, too. Well, I'm sorry, but that's not going to happen as long as "Dr. J" is alive and well. That would be me. I work with parents to clarify their expectations through written rules. In the long run, my experience has been that written rules help to increase compliance with parental expectations. This is especially true when the written rules and subsequent rewards and consequences are implemented correctly and consistently (i.e., "the two 'C' words).

Now that you have finished reading through the six philosophical underpinnings of FAMILY, let's quickly review the six statements in bold italic print:

1. The "real world" is ordered and structured and the lack of order and structure results in chaos.

2. A hierarchy of authority and a healthy respect for it is a vital part of making order and structure work effectively.

3. Authority flows downward; however, without checks, balances, and feedback there is an increased risk of developing a dictatorship (i.e., Absolute power corrupts - ask Adolph Hitler).

4. Families need to be ordered, structured and have a hierarchy of authority. Authority flows downward within families - not upward (i.e., Children must learn to respect authority - parents, teachers, police, clergy, etc.).

5. A parent's primary responsibility is to prepare their child(ren) for the "real world" which is ordered, structured and requires a healthy respect for authority.

6. Written rules help to clarify expectations which ultimately increases compliance and decreases inappropriate behaviors for most individuals.

If you agree with the philosophical underpinnings of FAMILY, please continue to read this book. If you don't agree with the philosophical underpinnings of FAMILY, please reread all six sections again. If after reading this section for a second time, you still don't agree with the philosophical underpinnings of FAMILY, please give this book to someone else who will benefit from reading it. This is America and you have the freedom to raise your children the way you want to. However, please ask them not to run for the office of the President of the United States. Presidents Nixon and Clinton were enough for one nation.

Important Definitions in order to Understand FAMILY

Throughout the years, I occasionally hear parents say something like, "This FAMILY system of yours sure sounds awfully rigid to me. I'm not sure if something like this will help us with our family problems." Although they were correct in implying that rigidity would not help their family through troubled times, they were incorrect in their assumptions that FAMILY is a rigid system. FAMILY is a flexible system. It is a living and breathing document. The rules are not chiseled in stone. The list of rules can be added to, deleted from, or modified at anytime. I'll explain more about this later in chapter eight. FAMILY provides order and structure for parents pertaining to their already existing rules and disciplinarian intervention strategies. FAMILY doesn't offer much of anything new. Instead, it helps to organize and structure what parents are trying to do in a much more effective way.

Let's take a closer look at a few key definitions that contribute to the philosophical underpinnings of FAMILY:

> **Order** - 1. A condition of logical or coherent arrangement among the individual elements of a group. 2. A. A condition of standard or prescribed arrangement among component parts, such that proper functioning or appearance is achieved. B. Systematic arrangement and design. 3. A. The established organization or structure of society. B. The rule of law and custom or the observance of prescribed procedure (Webster's II: New Riverside University Dictionary, 1994).

Simply put, FAMILY offers parents a logical arrangement for their family. It helps facilitate clear expectations and standards in order to achieve proper family functioning and appearance. FAMILY, by design, is systematic in it's arrangement. FAMILY helps prepare children for the established organization and structure of society. Children learn the rule of law and custom and how to observe prescribed procedures at home, school, church, synagogue, and in their community. Order is good. Order is not rigid. FAMILY is ordered - not rigid.

Let's take a look at another key definition that is a significant building block in the philosophical underpinnings of FAMILY:

> **Structure** - 1. Something made up of a number of parts held or put together in a specific way. 2. The manner in which parts are arranged or combined to form a whole. 3. Interrelation of parts in a complex entity. 4. Relatively intricate or extensive organization. 5. To give form or arrangement to. (Webster's II: New Riverside University Dictionary, 1994).

FAMILY assists parents by organizing their values and morals (expectations) in a specific way that forms a whole system of family structure. The system gives form or arrangement to what is often identified as "flying by the seat of their pants" (i.e., "parenting by ear"). Quite often, parents cross their fingers and pray that their children will survive adolescence. With FAMILY, parents can take a positive approach instead of "parenting by ear." FAMILY helps them organize and structure their approach to parenting. No more "flying by the seat of your pants" or "playing it by ear."

Just for the fun of it, let's take a peek at the definition for rigid/rigidity. Since some parents think there is a possibility that FAMILY might be too rigid for them, they should at least try and understand what rigid really means. The definition is as follows:

> **Rigid/Rigidity** - 1. Not bending: INFLEXIBLE. 2. Not moving: Stationary. 3. Difficult. Synonyms: stiff, unbending, unyielding. Core meaning: not changing shape or bending (rigid iron bars). (Webster's II: New Riverside University Dictionary, 1994).

FAMILY is anything but rigid. If you haven't figured it out by now in your reading, you will have it figured out by the end of the book. As previously stated, FAMILY is flexible and is a living and breathing document. It is not chiseled in stone. As long as both parents are in agreement, they can add rules, delete rules, and/or modify existing rules anytime they want to.

Once again, order and structure are not the same as rigid/rigidity. FAMILY provides order and structure but it is not rigid. FAMILY is a living and breathing document that can change over time. It bends, it's flexible, it moves, it's easy, and it changes shape as needed. If you think FAMILY is rigid, it is because you lack a proper understanding of the previous definitions and how they differ from one another. Structure and order are healthy and necessary to make the "real world" and families run smoothly. If you still can't see this, there is a possibility that you may have unresolved issues from your past with authority, structure and discipline that are interfering with your present ability to rationally perceive what I'm trying to convey. Consider addressing these issues in therapy before implementing any kind of parenting program.

Now, before we move on to the next chapter, we need to take a quick peek at a couple more definitions. FAMILY utilizes consequences for bad behaviors (e.g., Good Habit Cards), as well as rewards for good behaviors (e.g., FAMILY Tokens and RAK chips). Every once in awhile, I have a parent say the following concerning the rewards aspect of the system: "You're asking me to bribe my kid to behave. I shouldn't have to bribe my kid to do the right thing!" I couldn't agree more with the concerned parent. The very definition of the word, "bribe," means something completely different than the understanding the concerned parent is conveying. Bribe is defined as follows:

> **Bribe** - 1. Something, as money or a favor, offered or given to someone in a position of trust to induce him or her to act dishonestly (Webster's II: New Riverside University Dictionary, 1994).

The FAMILY system would never encourage parents to offer money or a favor to their children to induce them to act dishonestly. Quite the contrary, FAMILY encourages honest behaviors and seeks to move children in a positive direction toward conforming to their parents values and morals (i.e., expectations). I would never ask a parent to bribe their child. Reward their child, yes. Bribe their child, absolutely not!

Since the "R" word was brought up (i.e., reward), maybe we should take a quick peek at what the definition truly means:

> **Reward** - 1. Something, as money given or offered especially for a special service [i.e., involving honest behavior]. 2. A satisfying result (Webster's II: New Riverside University Dictionary, 1994).

Clearly, FAMILY encourages parents to reward, not bribe, their children for their good behaviors which bring about satisfying results for everyone involved. Happy children make for happy parents. Happy parents make for happy children. It's a never ending circle of familial bliss which is certainly better than the other conflictual option which many families experience.

In summary, compensating your children for good behaviors is not bribery. Adults are rewarded in their jobs by receiving paychecks, bonuses, awards, trips, raises, tips, promotions, recognition by the company, and other possible benefits. Likewise, children are rewarded for good behaviors by their parents. This is appropriate preparation for the real world. You'll never ever insist that your employer stop rewarding you for your good hard efforts on the job. Likewise, go therefore to your domicile and bless the buns of the fruit of your loins or womb (i.e., reward your children when they do good).

3   *The Struggles of Parenting*

The biggest challenge for parents is balancing the roles of disciplinarian and friend. Unfortunately, many parents favor one role over the other. Dads usually lean in the direction of disciplinarian and may or may not invest time and energy in the role of friend. Moms, on the other hand, tend to lean in the direction of friend while sacrificing the role of disciplinarian. How most parents choose to parent often depends on what was role modeled for them while growing up. Some parents like what they experienced growing up and try to repeat it with their own children. Conversely, other parents consciously attempt to raise their children in the opposite manner in which they themselves were raised.

Both roles, disciplinarian and friend, are important and must be utilized by both parents in the home. Although some parents don't like to hear this, the role of disciplinarian is primary while the role of friend is a very close second. Unfortunately, too many parents have a misconception as to what the role of disciplinarian really means. Some parents experienced abuse while being disciplined and automatically think that any form of disciplinary action should be avoided. In a sense, they are choosing to throw the proverbial "baby out with the bath water." I believe that they are understandably overreacting emotionally to past abuses and they do not understand the definition of disciplinarian which is defined as follows:

> **Discipline** - Training expected to produce a specific type or pattern of behavior, especially training that produces moral or mental improvement; A systematic method to obtain obedience; A state of order based on submission to rules and authority (Webster's II: New Riverside University Dictionary, 1994).

In spite of the past abuses I experienced while being punished, I clearly understand that the definition of disciplinarian does not involve the beating of a child with a belt, shoe, bat, fist, or 2x4, nor does it involve the pulling of hair, ears or lips, cigarette burns, cold water in a bathtub, or the verbal assault of the child. Rather, the word discipline comes from the root word, "disciple." To disciple a child means to guide, teach and instruct them in a manner which will help them stay on the straight and narrow path in life. Parents need to teach their children to stay between the lines on the road of life. The lines represent the rules they are to follow. Occasionally, parents need to be the guardrails for their children when they are nearing the dangerous curves in their early lives. Like most driving instructors, as parents, you hope that your child remembers to slow down for those dangerous curves along life's path after they are grown and leave your care.

A parent must be a disciplinarian first before being a friend. If the roles are reversed and the parent uses the democratic model, taking on the lower role of a sibling, the parent is undermining his or her own parental authority. Inevitably, the parent will have to put his or her foot down or draw a line in the sand. Sadly, the child will laugh at the parent and continue to disobey. After all, the child doesn't have to listen to the parent; he or she is just another sibling. However, the parent who is a disciplinarian first and, secondly, a very close friend, will have the respect of their children during the difficult moments in life. This type of parent is more apt to experience the desired outcome from the child during trying times because the child knows that the parent mean business. The child knows, without a doubt, that he or she will pay the piper for disobedient behavior. The fear of dad and mom is the beginning of wisdom. Fear is good. Reverent fear toward authority figures is a must and it begins at home.

For those of you who struggle with prioritizing these two roles, let's take a look at the definition of a friend:

> **Friend** - A person whom one knows, likes, and trusts; A person with whom one is allied in a struggle or cause; A supporter or sympathizer; Worthy of a friend; Warm and comforting; One fighting on or favorable to one's own side (Webster's II: New Riverside University Dictionary, 1994).

For those parents who struggle with the concept of friendship with their children, especially fathers, it really isn't that difficult to do; It just takes spending consistent time with your children. Just for the record, spending time with your children means doing what they want to do. This does not mean running errands with you. In other words, dad, inviting your children to go with you to the hardware store or auto parts store is probably not their idea of having a good time. Investigate how your children would like to spend time with you. This might include coloring, putting puzzles together, bike riding, surfing the Internet, going to a movie, fishing, shooting baskets, shopping, or going out for a hamburger. The point is, it takes consistent time to develop a friendship with your children and they need to know that you are willing to meet with them on their turf. You just might have to stretch yourself a little. Time spent with your children is time well invested; however, don't forget your primary role of being a disciplinarian.

If parents are really going to be friends to their children, they will admit they need to be a disciplinarian first and foremost. Children need to trust their parents to be allied with them in their developmental struggles in life. Children need to know their parents are fighting on their side in a supporting and sympathizing manner. Most important of all, children need to know that if their parents see them walking toward a cliff, they won't just stand there, smile, and wave goodbye. Rather, children truly want their parents to provide boundaries for them (i.e., order and structure). A primary disciplinarian becomes a true friend, one that is dependable and safe.

What's that? Are you laughing at what I just wrote? So you don't believe that children want structure, huh? That's "aye" for you Canadian readers. Do you want an example? Just read the letter to the editor found in the *Daily News Miner* published in Fairbanks, Alaska:

I'm Sorry - December 18, 1996

To the editor:

Today I turn 17. My cellmate wished me a happy birthday, but my outlook is still considerably less than jovial. Not only am I sad because I'll probably be spending the next 30 years of my life in prison, but I am ashamed of all the evil, rotten, and downright horrible things I have done to people.

I ripped off countless upstanding citizens, vandalized cars, garages and yards, and shot probably the finest member of the Alaska State Troopers.

I will say that I'm sorry to all those who I wronged. I will take responsibility for my actions. I will take this opportunity to make a public apology to Sergeant Roberts and his family who went through a terrible ordeal because of my stupidity and cruelty. I will say that I am not proud of anything that I have done, and that I never brag to any of the sick inmates here who commend me for my "bravery." Finally, I will get down on my knees every night for the rest of my life and thank God that I didn't kill that man.

That is all I can do. If that doesn't make anyone feel better, maybe the knowledge that the best years of my life belong to the state of Alaska will console them. I don't know.

What I do know is that something must be done about juvenile crime. There is probably one stoned kid in every classroom at West Valley [High School] during any given period. (I know, I was one of them.) Vandalism is out of control. Kids love to brag about how much damage they caused and theft and burglary have become more and more common.

More police would help. Stiffer penalties for first-time offenders are a must, extra youth activities might do some good, but the most important thing is families.

Talk to your kids. Find out where they are going and what they are doing. Do anything but please don't let them end up like me. Please.

David J. Knutson
Fairbanks Correctional Center

This young man's letter is crying out for structure. He is encouraging parents to recognize the fact that the family unit is the most important institution on the planet. David encourages parents to talk with their children, find out where they are going and what they are doing, and to do anything to prevent them from getting into trouble so they don't end up like him and become incarcerated. David Knutson was sentenced to prison for thirty years due to his actions which almost cost the life of Alaska State Trooper, Sergeant J.R. Roberts.

What? Okay, I get it. You're still unconvinced that children want their parents to provide them with structure even if they appear to be stating the opposite. Well, here goes another attempt at winning you over. I will discuss another example of parental inaction in the following paragraphs.

A former client in New Jersey, Linda, was a very popular girl in high school. She enjoyed the social scene like other teens at school. As a result, she ended up succumbing to various forms of peer pressure and engaged in experimentation with alcohol, marijuana, and sexual promiscuity. Linda was angry at her parents' unwillingness to set limits for her or confront her about her inappropriate behaviors. One time, Linda wrote a letter to her parents about the frustration she felt and left it by her bed, knowing her parents would find it. They found it, read it, and didn't do a thing about it. According to Linda, her parents were too afraid of how she might respond to their confrontation so they did nothing. "Parental paralysis" in action.

Linda continued with her anger and inappropriate behaviors. Eventually, while in college, she chose a different path. However, it took many years for her to get over her anger toward her parents' inaction. You're still not convinced that children want their parents to put their foot down? Didn't you read about Ed and Theresa in chapter one? Remember what they did? They brought their mom to see me due to her lack of consistency in implementing FAMILY. Okay, I recognize the fact that you need a little more convincing. Even if your child is looking you in the face and screaming, "I hate you! I'll never talk to you again," at the top of their lungs, they still want you to put your foot down and set limits for them. This will be my last attempt to convince you. Otherwise, I'll allow you to choose your path which will ultimately lead to your having to put up or shut up concerning your children's inappropriate behaviors because you're unwilling to do anything about it. Inaction is never productive or healthy.

Remember Carl in chapter one? Well lets take another look at his story. The saga continues. After his parents, Jason and Cathy, finally decided to send him to long-term residential treatment, they asked me to escort their son, and they made arrangements for his admission into the program in Western Samoa. I met Carl's parents to discuss the intervention strategies. I arrived at their home on a Sunday evening around 9:00 P.M. and went into the living room to talk with Carl. He was understandably surprised by my appearance. I talked with him about the fact that his parents love him and have tried everything under the sun to help him without success. I reminded Carl that he continually violated their expectations of him and that he was out of control. I informed him, that because of those choices, his parents had decided to admit him into a long-term residential treatment program in Western Samoa called Paradise Cove (www.wwasp.com).

Immediately, Carl became understandably upset and went into a tirade. He took physically aggressive steps toward his father, Jason, with raised closed fists. I was left with no other choice but to restrain Carl to the floor to help keep him and his parents safe. Carl immediately began to cry with deep sobs. Jason immediately got down on the floor with Carl and cried too, with his loving arms wrapped around him. This moment was truly difficult for all involved. I could tell that it was tearing Carl's parents' apart to put their foot down. I spent the night at Carl's home making sure that he didn't try to run away or harm himself. His mother, Cathy, called the Alaska State Troopers to inform them of our escort plans just in case they went sour. Fortunately, Carl got the point that I was following him around his home like a shadow and that he wasn't going to have a chance to flee on foot.

Therefore, Carl began to lobby his parents during the early morning hours to rescind their decision. He was not successful with his mother so he went into Jason's bedroom to emotionally twist his arm to no avail. At 5:00 A.M., Carl's pastor and a deacon from his church arrived. As we were leaving, Carl made one last attempt to get his parents to change their mind. He screamed and told them he hated them, what they were doing was wrong, and that he would never talk with them or see them again. His words were like a sharp dagger piercing his parent's heart. Carl's parents are to be admired and applauded for the love they demonstrated that day for the welfare of their son. They were willing to take the risk and put their foot down regardless of the threats. Carl's parents stayed at home while the pastor, deacon, and myself escorted him to the Fairbanks airport. We were met by the airport police and a friend of mine. At this point in time, Carl clearly understood he was headed for Western Samoa. There was no turning back.

When we landed in Seattle, Carl told me about all the fun things he was going to do with his father once he returned to Fairbanks, Alaska. He was looking forward to going out to their cabin on the boat. He told me several times how he needs to take care of his father and mother because no one else will. We were greeted by the Seattle airport police and escorted to a waiting room until our plane departed. Carl and I had a great talk about his behaviors and attitudes. He was willing to admit, for the first time, that he was out of control. When we landed in Los Angeles, Carl stated, "You know what? I think my parents made the right choice. I need to get some serious help. I think they are sending me to the right place." While Carl was sitting in a waiting room at the LA airport with a police officer, I called Cathy and informed her about Carl's statements. Cathy cried tears of joy and couldn't wait to tell Jason. I shed some tears too. When we arrived in Honolulu, Carl couldn't stop talking about Western Samoa and what it would be like; however, he made it clear to me that he was going to miss his snow boarding in Alaska. When we arrived in Western Samoa, Carl wanted to tour the island for a day and then go to the treatment center. Carl's words had changed from intense hatred, threatening never to see his parents again, to those of appreciation. For his personal well-being, Carl's parents were willing to put their foot down.

Eight months later, I provided another professional escort service for a 15-year-old boy from Fairbanks, Alaska to Apia, Western Samoa. Michael's escort provided me with an opportunity to personally check up on how Carl was doing. After Michael's admission to Paradise Cove was secured, I asked to meet with Carl. I waited with emotional reservation trying to anticipate how Carl would respond when he saw me. Carl walked briskly through the office door, he gave me the biggest and longest hug of my life. He ended the hug with an affectionate rubbing of the hair on my head. I was overwhelmed with joy and blown away by the look of mature serenity on his face.

While in Western Samoa, I was able to take Carl off grounds twice and spend time with him. He talked nonstop about everything he was learning about himself and his family while receiving treatment at Paradise Cove. Occasionally, he would shed tears of remorse when he would recall how he treated his family and how he treated himself. He thanked me numerous times for bringing him to Western Samoa. Most important of all, Carl never stopped talking about his love for his parents and his appreciation for the great deal of love it must have taken them to send him to Paradise Cove. He stated, "You guys saved my life. Thanks!"

Although I left Western Samoa feeling good about Carl's undeniable growth and progress, I couldn't help but feel the hurt and anger Michael was feeling by my leaving him behind for treatment. However, I am confident beyond a shadow of a doubt that Michael will also one day see the error of his choices and ultimately thank his parents and myself for what needed to be done on his behalf. Nevertheless, even if they deny it up front, children are always ultimately grateful when parents provide structure for them. Parents who spare discipline ultimately harm their children because sparing discipline is neglect. Neglect is abuse.

4

The Seven Cardinal Sins of Parenting

As you have learned in Chapter Three, and most likely have experienced, it is difficult to balance the two roles of disciplinarian and friend. Since I'm on a roll in challenging your thinking about parenting, let's explore the seven cardinal sins of parenting. You know, the seven guaranteed ways to undermine your own parental authority. The seven quick steps of assuring that you will lose the respect and control of your children; consequently, you end up living in misery for the next two decades of your life until your children are grown and gone.

1. Talking Too Much (i.e nagging, lecturing, etc.).

Have you ever watched a Charlie Brown cartoon? Do you remember the classroom scenes where the teacher talks nonstop? "Wha wha wha, wha wha wha wha. Wha wha wha wha, wha wha wha wha." As the teacher goes on and on and on and on and on, the Peanuts characters tune her out. Her lesson is going in one ear and out the other. Sound familiar?

It is absolutely amazing how quickly we as parents forget the important lessons from our own childhood experiences. Whenever one of my parents went into a lecture mode, within two minutes, I would tune them out. I figured, like most kids, that most of the important stuff was said already and the rest of the words were emotional filler material so they could feel better. Now look at us! Here we are, taking the same silly approach with our children that our parents used with us, and their parents used with them, and their grandparents used with their parents. It's a never-ending vicious cycle. A trans-generational curse. Stop the merry-go-round and let me off!

You can break free of the curse. You can decide right here and now to say what you need to say in only two or three sentences. Two paragraphs at the most. If your mouth can't stop talking, go see someone for help. Your children are intelligent and can quickly understand what you are trying to convey. Treat them as such. Expect as much. You will be surprised at the compliance you will gain from your children by stopping your tour on the lecture circuit. They will be more apt to listen to you the next time you have something to say to them.

2. Tirades and Temper Tantrums.

When was the last time you were the recipient of someone's tirade? I mean a good, old fashioned, in your face, red skinned, bulging jugular veins, bugged out eyes, ear drum piercing tirade, all just for your listening pleasure. Didn't you just love it? Secretly wishing you could experience a similar tirade on a daily basis? Didn't it make you feel loved unconditionally? No!!! It didn't!!! So why are you doing it with your children? What do you think you're going to accomplish by these angry outbursts besides having your children disrespect you, fear your presence, and think and see less of you when they are adults? When disciplining your child, never ever yell, scream, belittle, or cuss at them. You just simply don't do it.

When I was growing up, my father tried to teach me how to repair car engines and how to build various projects in the backyard. Initially, I liked being with my father. What kid doesn't? The demands of being a State Trooper kept my father away from home, so when he was home, I loved spending time with him. However, I quickly grew tired of trying to be his student because he would get mad so easily about insignificant issues. Accidentally, I would hand him the wrong tool from time to time. He would yell, "If your head wasn't screwed on, you'd lose it!" Sometimes he would say, "If you had brains, you'd be dangerous." Of course, there was the customary swear words and other put downs that always made those learning times memorable. Please don't get me wrong, I love my father and I still love to spend time with him; however, he now realizes that what he did with his anger toward us kids while we were growing up, was way out of line. He has since apologized profusely. I accepted his apologies, forgave him, and our relationship is healed.

When you are disciplining your child, you ought to treat the situation as if you are conducting business. Pretend you are a cashier behind a counter and Mr. Rude of America comes up to you and let's you have it verbally. As much as you probably want to, you don't punch him between the eyes or rip out his heart quick enough so he has a chance to watch it pump before he falls on the floor. Instead, you calmly listen to the customer and try to remedy the situation. Once again, when you are disciplining your child, pretend they are the customer and you are the cashier. Treat them politely and with respect. Get your point across without demeaning them and use as few words as possible.

I'm serious about this: if you can't get a handle on controlling your anger, then maybe you need to see a counselor in your community for anger management. Perhaps you need to be evaluated by a psychologist or psychiatrist for depression or a bipolar disorder (i.e., manic depressive disorder). Don't be too proud. If you have tried and tried to manage your own anger without success, then seek professional help. You are worth it, your spouse is worth it, and so are your children. It's better to work on resolving your problems now than to wait to say you're sorry later. How you treat your children today will have a strong impact on how they treat your grandchildren in the future.

3. Tears (i.e., sadness and guilt trips).

I'm not trying to be a sexist here, but the reality is that moms usually transgress in this department more often than dads do. When you feel like you have tried everything under the sun to get your children to cooperate and succeed in life, it's easy to become frustrated with them. Sometimes the frustration can feel so overwhelming that it can lead a parent to tears. While crying, and sometimes emotionally despondent, some mothers attempt to guilt trip their children into compliance. As a result, your children perceive you as weak and ineffective. They will not obey a whiny sniveling sibling.

You just successfully undermined your own parental authority. Never ever let your children see you as a broken down victim of their manipulation and disobedience. Rather, muster up enough strength, courage, and wisdom to save your tears for a private moment or leave your home and visit with a friend, counselor, or clergy. Like Connie, the single parent, in Chapter One, you must develop a parental backbone of steel instead of a wet spaghetti noodle. "I can't do it," is unacceptable. If Connie could do it, any mom can. You may need the assistance of a licensed counselor.

4. Terror (i.e., threats of violence).

When I was a young adolescent, my father more or less reminded me that he was an Oregon State Trooper and that if I ever did anything illegal, he would kill me and throw my rotting corpse in jail. This was the same Oregon State Trooper and father who arrested Santa Claus for trespassing and shot Rudolph the Red Nosed Reindeer on Christmas Eve in 1965. He told me that when I was four years old and I believed him. The stern look on his face when he warned me as an adolescent convinced me to never drink, do drugs, chew, or hang with those kids who do. Nevertheless, although his threats of violence were effective, they were also very inappropriate. There is a major difference between firm discipline with appropriate consequences versus physically threatening your child. Don't ever physically threaten your child. It's definitely not good for their psychological well being or good for relationship building.

Finally, never threaten to harm your kids physically because it is illegal in all 50 states and, most likely, the Child Protective Services agency will remove your children from your home. What's that I hear? You think I'm against corporal punishment? Absolutely not! I'm all in favor of corporal punishment for ages two through preschool. However, corporal punishment must be done in a controlled manner with predetermined guidelines. Parents need to understand their local and state laws and behave accordingly. Spanking should always be a last resort option used only after all other creative alternatives have been tried. Spanking should never occur when a parent is angry nor should it ever exceed one to three very light swats. It is never a good idea to use an object because it could injure your child and possibly leave marks and bruises. Marks and bruises mean that the Child Protective Services agency can intervene. Finally, spanking should never occur with kids in kindergarten or older. They are too old to spank. I don't care what other parenting programs teach you! Don't ever spank children in grades K-12. Please, trust me. FAMILY provides a much more effective approach to achieving desired behavioral outcomes for children in grades K-12.

The bottom line is that there is a major difference between threats of physical violence versus corporal punishment. Don't let well meaning providers of human service organizations tell you otherwise. Some of them attempt to argue that a young child doesn't know the difference between being physically beaten and abused versus receiving a spanking as an act of discipline. I certainly knew the difference when I was a kid, and so did you. I deserved my appointments with "Mr. Spanky" when I behaved inappropriately as a young child. I didn't deserve the abuse.

Research your state laws concerning corporal punishment at home and school. Contact the Attorney General's office in your state. Consult with your own attorney. Find out what your parental rights are. Don't roll over and play dead just because well meaning human services providers with good intentions are trying to cram their personal ideology down your parental throat. If you're really motivated, start a grass roots movement in your school, community, county, or State to protect parental rights. Above all else, don't ever physically threaten or physically abuse your children or you really do deserve to have them taken away from you.

5. Inconsistency (i.e., within and between parents).

Remember "the two 'C' words" mentioned in the beginning of this book (i.e., "correct and consistent" implementation of FAMILY)? Consistency is the crucial ingredient in being a successful parent. If you are unwilling to be consistent as a parent, hang it up. In reality, most of us would like to hang it up occasionally. We love our kids. We could just use an occasional vacation from them every now and then.

Parents need to consistently implement discipline in their home regardless of their mood or energy level. I don't care how hard your day was at work, if your child needs discipline, then do your job. I don't care how emotionally or physically exhausted you are, if your child needs discipline then do your job. However, never discipline in anger. If necessary, take a time out so you can discipline with a calm and rational approach.

All adults prefer consistently fair treatment from their supervisors. In return, do unto others as you would have others do unto you. Be consistent with your kids. Consistently give them rewards when they do right and consistently nail them to the proverbial wall when they do wrong. Children really appreciate consistency and structure.

Dads and moms, it's very important that you are consistent not only within yourself but also between one another. You can't have dad saying, "no", while mom is saying, "yes." You can't have dad restricting a child from the TV for a day, while mom grounds the child for a week for the same offense. This creates confusion for the children and conflict between the parents. It also sets dad and mom up to be manipulated by their kids. Under these circumstances, children learn to go to dad for some things, and to mom for other things. A house divided will not stand.

According to all the parents I have talked to, who choose to implement FAMILY in a correct and consistent manner in and outside of their home, the conflict of division between dad and mom has been eliminated. The conflict is eliminated because the rules, chores, rewards, and consequences are predetermined by both parents. If FAMILY is correctly and consistently implemented by both parents, there will be nothing to argue about concerning discipline. Parents really like it but some children are disappointed because they can't manipulate their parents anymore. Too bad, so sad.

6. Disagreeing about Discipline in front of the Children.

You must never allow your children to see you and your spouse openly disagree about how to discipline them. These discussions are reserved for private settings only (for example, the parents bedroom, a long walk or drive, etc.). When you have one parent displaying open disrespect for the other parent's authority, in front of the kids, you might as well declare open season on that parent. Like sharks, the children will smell the blood in the water and move in for the kill every time. The good news is that FAMILY helps to eliminate this problem and you will learn how in Part II of this book.

7. Treating your Children like They are Slaves (i.e., lack of reciprocity).

Lack of reciprocity in parent-child relationships creates major resentments among children. When parents demand much, but give little, insurrections can occur. Parents who are insensitive to their children's perception of fairness and credibility are asking for trouble. Although respect comes with the position of being a parent, you must behave appropriately to preserve the respect you desire from your children.

An example of this is the office of the President of the United States of America. In the minds of most U.S. citizens, respect for the office of the President is automatic. The office of the President is a national institution. If the President wants continued respect, he or she must continue to behave in a respectful manner. Otherwise, disgrace is brought to the office, whether Republican or Democrat. Just ask presidents Nixon and Clinton.

A good parent learns to lead by serving. A successful parent is sensitive to the needs of their children and seeks to meet them. As a result, the parent will reap what is sown. This will greatly increase the odds of raising children who are also sensitive to the needs of others. The acorn doesn't fall too far from the tree. Parents with a humble servant's heart raise children who eventually realize the fact that the world is not centered around them. There are other people on the planet with needs, too.

5

Reasons FAMILY Could Fail in Your Home

I HAVE TAUGHT FAMILY to physicians, attorneys, teachers, military officers, licensed mental health professionals, pastors, entrepreneurs, janitors, and plain old everyday All-American parents such as you and me. FAMILY has been developed with feedback from a thousand guinea pig families from New Jersey, California, Oregon, Washington, and Alaska. These families represent most religious, socioeconomic, ethnic, and cultural populations found in the United States. FAMILY has been well tested before reaching your home. If you are wondering whether or not you should try a variation or deviate from the way I am teaching you this system, please don't. Most likely, I have already been down that path with the previous 4,000 plus families. We have already been there, done that, and got the T-shirt (Don't forget to order your FAMILY Rules T-shirt at www.family-rules.com). I waited to write this book, after teaching FAMILY to a multitude of families. I wanted to make sure the system worked before writing a book about it, which would allow you to implement it in your own home. FAMILY works the way it is presented to you in this book, so please don't tinker with it or deviate from it.

I have seen FAMILY transform some of the most abusive home situations into a family environment where parents and children communicate and respect one another. Most recently, I taught FAMILY to a pastor and his family because they were having difficulty with an adolescent child. The children were not thrilled about the changes that were going to occur in their home once FAMILY was implemented. I warned them that life as they once knew it would cease to exist. I warned the family that changes were coming down the pike which would require an adjustment for everyone. Finally, based on my experience with multitudes of other families, I informed the children they were eventually going to be happy with the changes in their home and everyone would get along much better.

Approximately two months after I implemented the system with the pastor's family, I drove up to a window at a fast food restaurant in the community. While I was ordering edible materials to clog my arteries, the adolescent at the window stated, "I know you. You're the guy who implemented that FAMILY system with my family." I asked the adolescent, "So how is FAMILY working in your home?" The adolescent stated, "It's working really well. I had my doubts at first, but we are all getting along much better, just like you said. My parents are finally listening to me and I am finally listening to them. They are starting to let me do the things I want to do, because I'm finally following the rules. They trust me more than they did a while ago." As I drove away, I was very happy because I heard another success story about FAMILY and because I actually got everything in my bag that I ordered.

If you implement FAMILY correctly and consistently in your home (i.e., "the two 'C' words"), it will work; however, if you deviate from the way FAMILY is taught in this book, it will fail. In the spirit of beating a dead horse and recognizing that repetition is the best teacher, please read and reread this book to make sure you thoroughly understand the FAMILY system. You must implement the system correctly and, most important of all, consistently. If you don't implement FAMILY correctly and consistently, then it will fail in your home. Over the years, I have seen other reasons why FAMILY failed. I point these out in an attempt to help FAMILY succeed in your home. Please remember, correct and consistent implementation are essential ingredients for successful results.

1. See The Seven Cardinal Sins of Parenting (Chapter 4).

2. Parents are unwilling to put forth the time and energy necessary to implement FAMILY.

Parents truly expend much more time and energy trying to haphazardly manage the chaos in their home via "flying by the seat of their pants" than they would if they correctly and consistently implemented FAMILY in their home. Old habits die hard. Some parents are plain old lazy when it comes to disciplining their children and simply don't want to change. They would rather remain apathetic, inconsistent, or bark out commands from their armchair, while reading the paper and watching TV at the same time. In short, they'd rather not change their own lives, let alone involve themselves personally in changing the lives of their children.

The initial implementation of FAMILY in your home is very similar to pushing a stalled car out of a busy intersection. You know you need to move fast in order to avoid an accident; however, it takes a lot of energy at the beginning to get the car moving. You lean your shoulder into the rear of the car, dig your feet into the ground and push with everything you have. Slowly, the car begins to move. The more you push it, the faster it begins to move. Eventually, you find yourself not having to expend so much energy to keep the car moving. The same is true concerning the implementation of FAMILY in your home. Stay committed to "the two 'C' words" and your parenting job will be much easier down the road. If you give up and go back to "flying by the seat of your pants," you will create monsters and you will expend much more energy in the long run.

3. Parents are unwilling to practice what they preach (i.e., "Do as I say and not as I do.").

Life experiences, you would think, should stick in the memory banks of most adults concerning what they experienced as children growing up; however, they usually don't. I never liked it when my parents' actions clearly conveyed the message, "Do as we say, not as we do." I would ask myself, "If mom says smoking is bad for me, then why does she continue to smoke?" Also, "If mom says drinking is bad for me, then why does she drink so much?" The one word that came to my mind when I saw my parents behave this way is the same word that comes to the minds of most children when they see their parents provide this kind of role modeling – Hypocrite. I can really see the parents' minds spinning inside their heads when I ask them to stop swearing if they expect the same from their children. Most parents agree with the wisdom of consistent role modeling for their children; however, I remember one parent in the military who argued that his parents were "good citizens," even though they cussed like truckers. No offense intended, truckers. But this principle isn't about being a "good citizen." It's about being a consistent parental role model.

4. Parents have unresolved issues from their childhood concerning authority (e.g., past abuses, growing up with an anti-establishment attitude, etc.).

While teaching parents how to provide discipline to their children, major roadblocks sometimes block the path to successful parenting. One married mother, Lisa, had great difficulty saying "no" to her children or holding her kids accountable for their behaviors. After asking Lisa many questions about her past, she was willing to admit growing up in a rigid and abusive environment with a father who never let her do what she wanted to do. She made a commitment to herself to protect her own children from a similar experience. However, Lisa created other problems for her children as a result of being overly permissive. In fact, she was always running interference to protect her children from her father. Oops! I really meant to protect them from her husband (must have been a Freudian slip). You get the picture don't you? Lisa was treating her husband as if he were her father. Believe me, this interferes with parenting.

Don't forget about Todd and Kris in chapter one. They were the couple from the late 1960s and early 1970s anti-establishment era, who believed in the pursuit of alcohol, drugs, rock 'n roll, free love, and government protest. Living out these inappropriate philosophies of life in the 1990s interfered with their ability to effectively parent their son, David. Yet, they were blind to this truth and were unwilling to admit that they were contributing to David's academic demise. Denial is another obstacle to successful parenting.

5. Parents are engaged in a power struggle with one another and don't want to give up their illusion of control (i.e. they don't want to share authority, there is marital discord, etc.).

Monkey see, monkey do. Children who witness their parents fighting while growing up learn to do likewise as married adults. Some parents don't know how to involve themselves in a marital relationship without conflict. They engage in a dance of anger and control with one another. One treats the other as a child or as being mentally deficient. Of course no one knows any better than this individual how to run the home and raise the kids. As a result, verbal and/or physical abuse sometimes occurs. In many situations, the abuse trickles down to the children as well. Marital and family counseling is needed in these situations.

If your spouse is physically abusing you, please contact a professional counselor in your community immediately. Perhaps a crisis shelter. Most importantly, contact the police and press assault charges. Don't let your spouse talk you out of it. Acquire support from loved ones, church, synagogue, and your community. Don't let the abuse continue!

Sometimes, in the midst of power struggles, one parent may become apathetic and aloof over time. This parent may withdraw from both the spouse and children. It may take professional assistance to involve the aloof parent and to stabilize the marriage.

6. Parents misuse FAMILY to promote their own rigid agenda and then, when it blows up in their faces, they accuse FAMILY of being rigid rather than owning their own issues.

Rigid parents promote rigid discipline. Guns don't kill people, people kill people. Rigid parents who desire to control others will use any means possible to promote their own rigid agenda. They will contaminate, twist or distort anything in order to promote their own desires. FAMILY is not exempt from this reality. If you have a spouse who is behaving this way, please put FAMILY on hold and seek the assistance of a professional counselor - preferably a FAMILY Counselor (please see Appendix A).

7. Parents are struggling with their own unresolved mental health issues which interfere with their ability to correctly and consistently implement the system (e.g., depression, generalized anxiety, adult ADHD, alcohol and drug abuse, spiritual immaturity, marital problems, etc.).

The issues identified above are pretty self-explanatory. Parents are people too. They struggle with a variety of physical, spiritual, and mental health problems that can interfere with their ability to parent successfully. You know who you are. If not, listen to your spouse, he or she will let you know. Get help if you need it. Denial for a while is understandable. Denial forever is unacceptable.

Although I can write several chapters on unresolved mental health issues for parents, for the sake of brevity, I'll address the one issue that concerns me the most: anger management for fathers. In a nutshell, there are many fathers out there who think it's okay to yell, hit, and break things when they are angry at their spouse and/or children. These fathers may have had poor role modeling while growing up and, therefore, never learned how to express their hurt and anger appropriately. These fathers may also have a major depressive disorder, a bipolar disorder, or ADHD with serious impulsivity problems. These fathers need professional help. You know who you are. Please seek professional help before you lose your wife, children, and/or career. Stop blaming your wife. Start taking responsibility for your actions before it's too late. Please get some help now. Just do it!

6

Tactics Used By Children to Manipulate Authority

I HAVE WORKED WITH children, adolescents and their families for nearly two decades. They have taught me a lot over the years. I have learned the ins and the outs of manipulating adult authority. I was an adolescent once and utilized my own developed tactics during that time of my life. Like many adults, I personally got away with a few devious deeds in my past. I am sure my parents would drop dead if they ever learned the truth about their role model child. Naturally, as our parents once had to do when we were younger, we are now faced with raising children and adolescents of our own. We love and want the best for our children, just as our parents wanted the best for us. Now it is our turn to carry the baton of wisdom and experience.

Here is the problem: wisdom comes from experience and we don't have any previous experiences. Raising children is just as new for us as it was for our parents when we were born. It is wise to consult with our parents about what they did to raise us; however, their well-meaning advice doesn't always fit the needs of the changing times. Rest assured, there are foundational truths that transcend each new generation of children and adolescents. It is an undeniable fact of life, as certain as death and taxes, that children will manipulate adult authority to achieve their goals whether or not they are moral, ethical, legal, or safe. The following are tactics used by children and adolescents to manipulate adult authority.

1. Guilt Trips.

The first tactic that children and adolescents will use to manipulate their parents and other adult authority figures is guilt. Guilt is like a hot knife that quickly cuts through butter without resistance. Likewise, children will use guilt to quickly cut through the better judgment of parents without resistance. We all love our children and we want them to know that. It is tough when they start comparing us to Attila the Hun, Adolph Hitler, Joseph Stalin, or Sadam Hussein. Most parents desire to do a good job while raising their children and are curious about how they compare with other parents. Parents often question whether they are being too strict or too lenient. Unfortunately, parents don't always have ways of connecting with other parents. When they do connect with other parents, it is often over sports activities, church or synagogue activities, community activities, or other activities that normally bring the community together. During these community events, the focal point of discussion is not based on whether or not parents are being too strict or lenient as compared to other parents, rather the discussion is focused on the specific event that brought everyone together.

Fortunately, there are parent support groups developing around the country so the focal point of the discussion can be on how to parent one's child. If you do not have a local parent support group, why not start one at your local school, church, synagogue, hospital, or community library? You can also join the FAMILY Rules discussion forum at www.family-rules.com and converse with parents from all over the world. Although it helps to know how you fit in with other parents in your community, ultimately, you are the ones who decide what your children may or may not do. If the majority of parents in your community believe it's okay for their children to be out until 1:00 A.M., but you would rather have yours home by 10:00 P.M., then your children will be home by 10:00 P.M. Don't allow your children to push your guilt buttons to cause you to go against your better judgment. Also, don't forget, your primary role as a parent is one of disciplinarian. First, you must paint the lines on the road of life and act as the guard rails on the dangerous curves, and second, you are a close friend. Don't let your children guilt-trip you out of your role as disciplinarian. When children and adolescents want something really bad, they will try to get you to be their friend first and disciplinarian second. This is a fatal mistake and you must not let it happen. No! No! No!

Remember Carl from chapter one? He was very good at manipulating his parents and he definitely knew how to push their guilt buttons. When his parents were talking with him in therapy about the possibility of sending him to a long-term residential treatment facility, he would automatically raise abandonment issues. In the past, they sent him to a snow boarding school in the lower 48 states without much success. In my humble opinion, the program did not sound very structured, nor did it sound very thorough in it's approach to treating children with emotional issues and behavioral problems. Carl would also raise issues of abandonment related to adoption. I observed his mother's body language and facial expressions as she would back off from her stance. I saw Carl and his mother cycle in and out of this dance in my office on a few occasions. It wasn't until Carl crossed the line, one too many times, with his mother that she finally decided, along with her husband, to send Carl to Western Samoa for long-term residential treatment. She was no longer going to allow Carl to push her guilt buttons and prevent her from doing what she knew she had to do to save his life. While in Western Samoa, during my third escort to the South Pacific island, I had a chance to spend more time with Carl. He openly admitted to me with remorse about how he would push his mother's guilt buttons to avoid being sent away. Carl was glad that his mother finally put her foot down and took care of business. Carl believes that his mother and father saved his life.

2. Divide Authority and Conquer.

A house divided cannot stand. These words are often attributed to President Lincoln; however, these words came from Jesus Christ when he was accused of being possessed by Satan. Jesus Christ more or less argued that he could not be possessed by Satan while at the same time doing the work of God (i.e., casting out demons). A house divided will not stand. Unfortunately, I have worked with families where children have successfully divided their parents. As years pass, certain relational patterns develop where both mom and dad believe that one parent is the good guy, while the other parent is the bad guy. Naturally, it is the other parent who is the bad guy. The problem with this approach to parenting is the fact that the house is divided and it will not stand. Therefore, the children get to sneak out the back door or side window and get away with murder, while mom and dad are verbally assaulting one another. Divorced parents are at high risk for being vulnerable to this tactic of manipulation. For some parents, the divorce and the reasons leading up to it have already convinced them in their own minds that the other parent is indeed, possessed by Satan (i.e., the bad guy). It doesn't take much convincing via a child's manipulation to confirm in one's own mind that their divorced spouse is indeed Satan incarnate. The sad truth is that some children of divorced parents know this and will use this tactic as many times as necessary to get their own way.

Jim and Cheryl divorced many years ago. Their son, Steve, lived with his mother for many years. As Steve grew older, he hooked up with a group of negative peers. His mother and new stepfather began to make more rules around the home to contain his inappropriate behaviors. Steve was not pleased with his mother's strictness, so he emotionally manipulated his father, Jim, and his new stepmother, so he could go live with them. Steve stayed with his father and new stepmother for almost one year until he burned his bridges with them. By the end of the year, his mother, Cheryl, had forgotten all the negative manipulations that Steve did in her home, and was convinced by Steve that her ex-husband, Jim, was indeed Satan incarnate (i.e., the bad guy). Therefore, Cheryl rescued Steve and brought him back home to live with her. Everything went fine for a few weeks until the honeymoon period was over.

Steve's new stepfather found his credit cards in Steve's pocket. Steve was going to use the credit cards to obtain cash advances in order get money for drugs. Cheryl and her new husband called up Jim and told him that he would have to take Steve back into his home. Jim and his new wife contacted me and set up an appointment to help them with the transition. Jim and his wife along with Cheryl and her husband came into my office for an appointment. Cheryl and her new husband made it clear that they did not want Steve back in their home. They were willing to give their 100%

cooperation to Jim and his wife. They signed a contract supporting Steve's presence in Jim's home and their willingness not to
interfere with any therapeutic recommendations made by myself.
Cheryl and her new husband also agreed that if Steve came running back to them, whining and complaining about how Jim was
Satan incarnate, they would direct him to go back to Jim's home
and work it out. They were no longer going to enable Steve with
his manipulations.

I had managed to help Jim and Cheryl paint their son, Steve, into a
corner that he could not get out of. Steve was left with only two
options: Follow the rules at home and school and enjoy an abun-
dant life, or disobey the rules at home and school and go to long-
term residential treatment. When confronted in my office by Jim
and myself, Steve chose to obey the rules at home and at school.
Unfortunately, it only took approximately four weeks for Jim and
me to realize that Steve's commitment to following the rules was
merely lip service. As a result, Steve chose to go to long-term residential treatment. As Steve was leaving my office, he told me that
he was glad he was going because he felt like his life was out of
control. He wanted help in getting a handle on his life and getting
his feet back on the ground. I told you so! Children and adolescents really do want organization, structure, and discipline. They
want to know that you will keep them safe no matter what.

3. Anger.

If guilt trips or dividing authority does not work, then children will
turn up the heat by utilizing the tactic of anger to manipulate their
parents. If I received a nickel for every time I heard about how a
child has attempted to manipulate their parents with anger, I would
be a wealthy man. Children and adolescents will slam doors, break
things, stomp their feet, punch, kick, scratch, bite, shove, or scream
at the top of their lungs with a red face and bulging eyes as they
walk towards you with clinched fists. Anger can be a very intimi-
dating emotion, especially when you have been the victim of verbal and/or physical abuse in the past.

What is a mother to do when she is confronted with the anger of
an adolescent son who is taller and heavier than she is? Sure, dad

comes home and tries to intimidate the adolescent son with his anger and the possibility of his physical confrontation. Eventually mom is left to fend for herself when dad is not around the home. Many mothers live in fear of their adolescent child's anger. Some mothers may attempt to counter their child's anger with their own anger and overreact in order to regain control in their home.

I recall attempting to utilize the tactic of anger with my own mom when I was an adolescent. She slapped me, grabbed my hair, dragged me up the stairs, threw me in my bedroom, and slammed the door shut behind me. She did what she thought she needed to do to get control over the situation. Today, that would be considered child abuse. It is important not to allow your children's anger to intimidate or manipulate you. Don't let them use anger to get their own way. It is also inappropriate for any parent to attempt to intimidate their children back and engage in physical abuse to regain control of the situation. You want to avoid the intervention of the Child Protective Services agency if at all possible. If they enter your world, they'll be like a wart on your foot that you can't get rid of to save your life. However, the Child Protective Services agency is a necessary evil. Who else will protect and advocate for the abused and neglected children in our communities?

Joel was out of control and a very angry adolescent. He intimidated his parents often into getting his own way. No matter how many times I attempted to persuade his parents to put their foot down and no longer tolerate Joel's outburst, they feared drawing a line in the sand. I warned them on numerous occasions that Joel's anger and manipulations were going to cost them greatly, one way or another, if they did not put their foot down immediately. One night, Joel's parents had a confrontation with him about his desire to go out with his friends on a school night. Joel was mad because his parents were going to go out on a date while he had to stay home and do his homework. Joel tried to use anger, but to no avail. When his parents came home, they found their living room and dining room furniture smashed to pieces. Joel had caused approximately $10,000 worth of destruction in their home. His parents called me in a crisis and decided it was time to send Joel to long-term residential treatment. His behaviors were obviously out of control and they needed more help than they were able to get in an outpatient treatment setting. This was obviously a "pop fly" and very deserving of an immediate admission into a long-term residential treatment center. You will read about "pop flies" in chapter eight. Joel was put on a plane and escorted out of Alaska down to the lower 48 States by his father for treatment. Anger can be a very destructive emotion if left unchecked. Parents must never allow their children to intimidate them with anger in order to get their own way. Parents must also not confront anger with anger, otherwise, they will merely escalate the situation by adding fuel to the fire. If necessary, take a time-out, calm down, then discipline your child.

4. Fear.

When all else fails, children and adolescents will pull out the thermonuclear warheads. The conventional warfare tactics of guilt, dividing authority, and anger have been unfruitful. Therefore, children and adolescents are now prepared to totally annihilate the enemy. Kids will attempt to intimidate their parents through fear by threatening to beat them up, kill them, hurt themselves, kill themselves, withdraw their love, run away from home, or go to school and shoot their peers. Parents must take all these threats very seriously and respond accordingly. For example, if your child threatens to harm themselves or someone else, you must immediately take them to your local psychiatric hospital or emergency room at your general hospital for a psychiatric evaluation. If your child refuses to cooperate by going to such a facility, you do have the option of contacting your local police to come over to your house and perform a safety check to make sure your child is not a danger to self or others. If necessary, the police should be able to transport your child to the appropriate mental health facility for safety and a psychiatric evaluation.

By taking all threats seriously and responding accordingly, your child will quickly learn that you care. You are not willing to allow him or her to commit harm to self or anyone else. Do not stop with your goal of getting your child evaluated, even if while on the way to a local psychiatric hospital, the child admits that he or she was only kidding. Send a message that you will take each threat seriously and respond accordingly. This will make your child think twice in the future before ever stating anything similar again.

I cannot over state the importance of taking each threat seriously. I can recall parents who did not take their daughter's threat of suicide seriously. They thought she just wanted attention. Sadly enough, one day her mother came home from work and found her dead due to an overdose of medication. I don't have any doubt there are kids who will use threats of suicide as an act of attention-seeking and manipulation; however, you never know if your child will be the one individual who really meant what was said. Therefore, once again, take all threats of harm to self and others seriously and act accordingly. Take a child to the hospital and if you do not have cooperation, call the police for a safety check. You must keep your child safe and send a message that you will not be manipulated with such tactics.

Fear is a pretty effective tool of manipulation. During my junior year of high school, we had just completed our basketball season in the State playoffs. Our season record was 25 wins and 1 loss. We took fourth in the state and had a very successful season. However, that wasn't the way I thought or felt about it. As a matter of fact, I was very depressed as a result of losing the one game during the State playoffs, which cost us the opportunity to play for the State championship. Fourth place wasn't good enough for me. In my mind, fourth place really meant third place looser. At that point in my life, having been raised in a dysfunctional family, my role was one of an over-achiever. Well, we lost. Losing was not achieving. In my mind, I let down my family, school, and community of Salem, Oregon. To cope with my dysfunctional family environment, I became basketball and I lost, therefore, I was very depressed.

After the Oregon State playoffs in March of 1979, I did not want to go back to school and face my peers and teachers. Now in reality, I am sure my peers and teachers didn't really care about whether or not we played in the championship game. After all, the fact that we made it to the State playoffs allowed my peers to miss many days of school and they were able to travel to Portland, to support us while we played our games. Nevertheless, in my dysfunctional adolescent mind, I was a loser and let them all down. As a result of my stinking thinking, I told my parents I needed time to get away and think. I informed them that I was depressed and I didn't know what I would do if I didn't have time to get away and think. Did you catch the subtle manipulation using the threat of fear? Well, mom and dad swallowed the bait, hook, line, and sinker. I got to miss school for a week.

My parents allowed me to drive to Seaside, Oregon and spend a week with our family friends. I drove the two-hour trip in approximately an hour and twenty minutes. Along the way, I almost killed myself by attempting to drive my parents' Pinto into a bridge. Fortunately, by God's grace, I did not do it. I pulled out of it at the last second. My parents did not take my threat seriously, nor act accordingly. What they should have done was take me to a therapist or a psychiatric hospital for a psychiatric evaluation. During that brief period in my life, I was very depressed and suicidal. As a result of their unwillingness to act accordingly to my threat, they almost had the unfortunate experience of having an Oregon State Trooper call them to inform them of a fatal auto accident involving their son. I am sure they thought they were doing the best thing by letting me go, but the best choice would have been to have me evaluated by a mental health professional. Rest assured, I am much more emotionally stable today. I would no longer consider killing myself over losing a game of basketball or for any other reason.

7 Childhood Struggles That Interfere With Compliance

SOMETIMES, A CHILD'S lack of compliance with adult authority at home and at school is not solely due to willful disobedience. A child might be struggling with other issues in life that, when combined with willful disobedience, make compliance with authority almost impossible. When a child has a disability, impairment, or disorder, it is not uncommon for parents to attribute all of the child's problems to a negative attitude problem. Sometimes parents may even conclude that these problems have their roots in spiritual matters.

I remember one day when Oprah brought her niece, Felecia, into my office for counseling. She had moved her niece up to Alaska from an urban environment in the lower 48 states. Oprah wanted to remove her from the influence of gangs. While Felecia was under her aunt Oprah's care in Alaska, they began to butt heads over different issues. Oprah brought Felecia into my office and requested that I exorcise the demon from her niece. I told her that if those were the services she desired, she would be better off pursuing an exorcism with the guidance of her pastor. I also explained to her that insurance companies don't reimburse for exorcisms performed by a psychologist.

Oprah was upset with me and demanded once again that I exorcise the demon from her niece. I utilized the initial one-hour diagnostic interview to ask her questions as to why she thought her niece, Felecia, was possessed by a demon. She began to explain many of her behaviors and symptoms to me. At the end of our session, I suggested that we proceed with psychological testing to rule out possible learning disabilities, attention deficit/hyperactivity disorder, and possible neuropsychological impairment. She stormed out of my office with Felecia in hand. Oprah was mad at me because I refused to exorcise the demon from her niece.

Two weeks later, Felecia and Oprah had a major blow out. Oprah admitted Felecia into the psychiatric hospital where I frequently performed psychological evaluations on adolescent patients. I was able to administer the psychological tests to Felecia that I had recommended earlier. The testing results indicated Felecia had a severe attention deficit disorder to auditory stimuli. She also had a moderate level of inattention problems to visual stimuli. In addition to these struggles, Felecia was also mildly mentally retarded, and she had some neuropsychological problems in the frontal lobe of her brain. This part of the brain manages abstract reasoning, problem solving, goal setting abilities, and emotional regulation.

After I wrote up my report, I sat down with Felecia's aunt, Oprah, and explained to her what Felecia was really dealing with. I shared with her how she could help Felecia compensate for her disabilities. I gave Oprah new ideas for parental interventions, such as writing down her directives, because nothing she said to Felecia ever stuck in her brain. The words Oprah spoke to Felecia in the past went in one ear and out the other due to her inability to pay attention to auditory stimuli. The psychiatrist also placed Felecia on Ritalin. A few weeks later, after Felecia's discharge from the hospital, Oprah called me and thanked me for the psychological evaluation and the parenting intervention tips. She stated that she and Felecia were getting along better now and that she did not appear to have a demon in her after all. I think Oprah finally caught on to the fact that sometimes people are so heavenly minded, they are of no earthly good. Although I believe in the spiritual realm, I just believe most of the problems that we face from day to day are the results of our own emotional, psychological, physical, and relational dysfunctions.

The following childhood struggles which might interfere with compliance to your authority are provided to help you screen for possible "red flags". If your child has one or more of these problems, please have them assessed by a licensed mental health profes-sional such as a psychiatrist, psychologist, or clinical social worker.

1. *Learning Disabilities.*

Most parents want to believe that their child is the best looking and smartest kid on the planet. We want to believe this is a fact of life and that our parental biases have nothing to do with our conclusions. However, 70% of all children fit somewhere within the average range - between the low end of the average range and the upper-end of the average range. Nevertheless, average is average. There are children who exceed the average range and excel above their peers. These children are either the valedictori-ans at high school graduation or troublemakers in the principal's office because they are so bored with school they don't know what else to do with their time.

Unfortunately, there are children at the other end of the spectrum who struggle with learning from day to day. Sometimes, these children are not always easy to spot. Children may excel in some subjects at school and struggle in other subjects. They may study for many more hours than their peers just to bring home a "C" grade. Some children sincerely put forth a lot of effort and man-age only to bring home a "D" or an "F" grade.

Once again, as I mentioned earlier, some parents will attribute negative motivations or reasons for why a child brings home a "D" or an "F" grade. In some cases they are right. In other cases they are wrong. There is such a thing as a Mathematics Learning Disability or a Disorder of Written Expression. Let's face it, the public school system is overwhelmed by the sheer number of students. Unless your child's academic struggles stick out like a sore thumb, you will need to advocate on his or her behalf with your school district. If you have any reason to suspect that your child is struggling with an academic learning disability, then you will need to approach your school to have your child evaluated. Please remember that the squeaky wheel gets the oil. Don't ac-cept "no" for an answer. The school district should be able to provide the Woodcock-Johnson Psycho-Educational Test Battery (WJ-III) to rule out one or more possible learning disabilities. If you have advocated strongly for your child and the school district is still unwilling to test him or her, then contact a local psychologist in your community and ask if he or she is trained to administer the WJ-III to your child. If a local psychologist identifies one or more learning disabilities via the appropriate testing, then you can go back to your school district armed with the necessary data to force them to test your child as you previously requested.

2. Intellectual Impairment.

There is a lot of controversy over whether or not an intelligence quotient (IQ) really exists. Well, let's settle this controversy once and for all. There is such a thing as an IQ. Just talk to Albert Einstein or David Hawking. Then talk to your uncle, Bubba. See what I mean? My experience over the years tells me that it is important to have an understanding of what your child's IQ is really like. One thing is certain, I really doubt that any individual can accurately guess what someone's IQ score is. I recall working in a psychiatric hospital with a psychiatrist who wanted me to administer an IQ test to an adolescent female. He estimated that her IQ was in the below average range and wanted a confirmation of this fact. I tested her as he requested and her IQ score turned out to be in the superior range. The psychiatrist was flabbergasted and couldn't understand how she obtained such a high score. After all, in his mind, this adolescent female had made nothing but one stupid mistake after another to get herself admitted into the hospital. He was certain that her IQ score was in the below average range and felt threatened that the IQ test pointed out otherwise. How in the world could he be wrong? After all, he was a medical doctor and a psychiatrist on top of that.

To be fair to the psychiatrist, in spite of the fact that I have administered many IQ tests, I too will occasionally try to guess, in my mind, what someone's IQ score might be before I administer the test; however, I learn that in most cases I am not right at all. I always chuckle when I read a report from another professional in the community who adds an estimate of an individual's IQ. I know from my own experience that there is no way on earth their estimate is an accurate one. Nevertheless, I do believe in the value of IQ testing and the data that it provides for the parents and educators. If we know a child's true IQ score, rather than just an inaccurate educated guess, we can adjust our expectations accordingly.

3. Attention Deficit/Hyperactivity Disorder (ADHD) and Attention Deficit Disorder (ADD).

There is a lot of misinformation circulating on the Internet, in the media, and in books about ADD/ADHD. Please remember, in spite of all the negative media sensationalism, bad news sells. For example, thousands of jet aircraft take off and land safely every day around the world. It is much safer to fly than it is to drive a car. Nevertheless, when one jet aircraft crashes we hear about it nonstop on all of the news channels for the next week or two. Was it pilot error? Was it a bomb that exploded? Was it mechanical failure? The cameras keep on rolling, reporters keep on asking questions, and the majority of the people keep on soaking it up. What we don't hear about or see on the TV news on a daily basis are scenarios such as this: "Here we are at Gate B-5 witnessing another successful passenger jet landing! Wait just one moment, I think I hear the passengers walking up the ramp. Yes! Here they are! More families reunited again and again!" The bottom line is, in spite of the negative media sensationalism, ADD/ADHD really does exist. For every negative story you can tell me about Ritalin or other psychostimulant medication, I can tell you a thousand positive stories about how the medication has helped individuals and families. Research studies show that the best way to treat this disorder is with a combination of medication and behavior modification working together, not one without the other. It's a good thing you are learning about the FAMILY system.

There has been a lot of hype about the over-diagnosing of ADD/ADHD in America. Granted, there probably have been individuals diagnosed with ADD/ADHD that do not have it. Likewise, others were not diagnosed with ADD/ADHD when they really did have the disorder. The most common way to diagnose ADD/ADHD in America is through a medical doctor. Unfortunately, although they are trained as physicians, their evaluation methods are very subjective at best. In other words, they ask a lot of questions or gather information on paper from teachers and parents. This method of gathering data is influenced greatly by the physician's bias, parental bias, and teacher bias. This means that the odds go up significantly of obtaining a false positive or a false negative diagnosis.

I am not minimizing the importance of obtaining subjective data, rather, I am pointing out the importance of obtaining objective testing data as a supplement. Objective testing options exist to identify the possible diagnosis of ADD/ADHD, but many physicians and psychologists are unaware of this fact. While conducting an assessment for ADD/ADHD, I administer the Wechsler Intelligence Scale for Children – Third Edition (WISC-III); Connors' Rating Scales for Parents and Teachers; the Test of Variables of Attention - Visual and Auditory (TOVA); and the Wisconsin Card Sorting Test. I also utilize the subjective information I glean from the initial one-hour diagnostic interview. The TOVA test and the Wisconsin Card Sorting Test are administered via a computer and the objective testing data is combined with the subjective data to reach a final diagnosis of whether or not the child, adolescent, or adult actually has ADD/ADHD. A thorough evaluation will use the best of both worlds – subjective and objective data.

Please be cautious while seeking evaluations for ADD/ADHD from physicians, psychiatrists, or psychologists who only utilize subjective data to formulate a diagnosis. Relying solely on subjective data that can be greatly influenced by the biases of a parent, teacher, or professional is not the best approach. Ask them about what objective tests they utilize in their diagnostic procedures to supplement their subjective data. Unfortunately, some of these professionals won't even know what you are talking about when you ask this question. Most of the hype out there in the media about misdiagnosis of ADD/ADHD is due to the lack of objective testing to supplement subjective information gathered by a professional.

A while ago, I had a young adolescent male, Paul, referred to me by a private school principal and his parents for an evaluation for ADD/ADHD. They were certain that he had this disorder. After giving him the tests that I previously described, it turns out that he was not even close to having ADD/ADHD. However, the objective testing data indicated the possible presence of depression, mild mental retardation, and the possibility of neuropsychological impairment. After additional testing, I was able to conclude that Paul was mildly mentally retarded and was experiencing a major depressive disorder. We were able to treat his depression, with the appropriate medication and counseling, and I referred him on to the public school system for special resource services. Although Paul was referred for ADD/ADHD, it turned out that his problem was altogether different. I believe that the subjective data combined with the objective testing data helped me to clearly differentiate between what Paul's parents and principal thought he was struggling with versus what he was really struggling with.

Finally, some school districts do a poor job of assessing and referring children and adolescents for evaluations for ADD/ADHD. I have lived in a community where the school district policy position concerning ADD/ADHD referrals was the same as President Bill Clinton's policy with gays in the military: "Don't ask - Don't tell." In this community, teachers often came up to me during my seminars and explained that they have been told, by the school district, not to tell a parent directly that their child needs to be evaluated for ADD/ADHD. Due to their interpretation of federal law, school district personnel believed it would be financially obligated to pay for the evaluation if the referral was made by a teacher.

When I attempted to talk about this with the school district superintendent and board members, I was told that teachers are not diagnosticians. They are not qualified to make such referrals. I chuckled and said, "So, if a child falls off of the playground equipment and breaks his arm, your teachers or school nurse won't make a referral to the emergency room to have the broken arm tended to because they are not professional diagnosticians?" The position of not making referrals for evaluations was a silly one, based on their fear of having to pay for the evaluation. My frustration with the school district heightened because I was dealing with the kids who were falling through the cracks. Children and adolescents with un-diagnosed and untreated ADD/ADHD end up having academic struggles and disliking school. Their self-esteem starts to dive and they manage to hang out with other adolescents in a similar state of existence. With their mutual dislike for school and the authority figures that constantly put them down for their academic failures, they decide to spend more of their time experimenting with alcohol and drugs. I end up having to treat these kids when they are in their late adolescent years. After conducting my initial one hour diagnostic interview, I see "red flags" all over the place for possible ADD/ADHD. I end up evaluating the child for the disorder and confirming the reality that they have it when they should have been evaluated years ago. Now the parents and I have to work over time to get the child's feet and self-esteem planted back on the ground. We end up putting Humpty Dumpty back together again while the school district has saved itself some money.

It is very important that you explore your local school district policy concerning referrals for ADD/ADHD evaluations. Some school districts will identify and refer for evaluations while other school districts adopt a "Don't ask - Don't tell" policy. Don't assume your child is in safe hands and that your school district will tell you when they think there is a problem. To be fair to some school districts, we do live in a litigious society and they do have some legitimate concerns of fearing they would have to pay for making a referral for such an evaluation. You can work with your local school board members and school district administration in creating a policy of assurance where referrals can be made without threat of payment. Create a grass-roots effort and get the ball rolling. We started a grass roots movement and succeeded in opening up the doors to permit teachers the freedom to talk openly with parents. The best books to read about ADD/ADHD are *Driven To Distraction* and *Answers to Distraction* both by Hallowell and Ratey. Learn about the real facts and toss Grandpa Stewart's and Aunt Betty's opinions into the garbage can.

4. Depression.

As time passes, we are learning more about the disorder of depression. Depression can definitely interfere with a child's ability to comply with adult authority at home or at school. Depression can affect one's self-esteem, energy level, and motivation, as well as the ability to pay attention and think clearly. Depression can be situational, such as in being brought on by the death of a loved one. Depression can be caused by one's geographical local such as the northern climates in Alaska, Canada, Europe, and Asia. Seasonal affective disorder is brought on by the lack of sunlight hitting the retina. As a result, a message is sent to the hypothalamus, which relays a message down to the pineal gland stating, "Hey, it's winter up here! It's time to hibernate!" People end up becoming grouchy, hungry, depressed, and they want to hibernate. Finally, depression can be caused by a biochemical imbalance in the brain. It is a well-documented fact that depression can be found in families due to a genetic predisposition. In other words, if you have one or both parents that have a history of depression, more than likely one or both of their parents had a history of depression. You or your child might end up experiencing a depressive disorder, too.

The best way to treat situational depression is through emotional support and time. The best way to treat a seasonal affective disorder is with a combination of an antidepressant and light-box therapy. Finally, the best way to treat a chemically imbalanced depression in the brain is with an antidepressant and therapy. It is best not to diagnose your children or yourself, rather, it is best to see a physician or a mental health professional for an evaluation.

5. Generalized Anxiety.

Anxiety is a real disorder and can be difficult to live with. It may cause children to disobey parental authority because they are trying to avoid facing their own fears and anxiety. They may not want to tell you about their anxiety or they may not even be consciously aware of their own anxiety and fears. Fortunately there is help for anxiety disorders. The best way to treat anxiety is with a combination of therapy and anti-anxiety medication. I believe the best therapeutic approach for treating anxiety is with a therapist who utilizes a cognitive-behavioral approach. In many cases, I believe, irrational and unhealthy thinking leads to problems with anxiety. When I help an adolescent or adult change their irrational thoughts to rational thoughts, more often than not, the anxiety eventually subsides. Eventually, they can go off their anti-anxiety medication and remain stable over time. Once again, don't diagnose your children or yourself, rather, see a physician or a mental health counselor for an evaluation.

6. Alcohol and Drug Abuse and Dependency.

More often than not, children with attitude problems toward authority figures at home and at school have experimented with alcohol and drugs on at least one occasion. I stopped being surprised years ago when a child would eventually confess to using alcohol, marijuana, or other illicit chemicals. Seldom will an adolescent confess to their parents or therapist about their use of alcohol and other drugs. If and when they do, they often under-report their usage.

Two good personality profile tests that I utilize as a psychologist to evaluate the adolescent clients that I work with are the Minnesota Multiphasic Personality Inventory for Adolescents (MMPI-A) and the Millon Adolescent Clinical Inventory (MACI). Not only are these the two most commonly administered personality profile tests for adolescents used in the United States of America, but they are probably the two most commonly administered personality profile tests used for adolescents in the Milky Way Galaxy. However, I have not talked to many extraterrestrials to confirm this fact. Nevertheless, these tests are adequate psychometric assessment tools used to compare your adolescent child's responses with other adolescent children.

These tests help determine whether or not your child is experiencing depression, anxiety, eating disorders, low self esteem, family discord, peer insecurity, and body discomfort. They also help ascertain whether or not your adolescent child is experimenting with alcohol and drugs or at least have the personality makeup of those who might be experimenting with alcohol and drugs. If I were you, and I thought my adolescent child was messing around with alcohol and other drugs, I would take my child to a psychologist and have these two tests administered. I would also take my child to get a urinalysis to see whether or not the urine is "clean."

Finally, you should know that the best approach to treating alcohol and drug abuse as well as dependency is in a group setting. Individual therapy with an alcohol and drug abuser is not as successful as group therapy in an outpatient or inpatient treatment setting. It is much tougher for the alcohol and drug abuser to pull one over on a group of people than it is to pull one over on an individual therapist.

As a side note, it is unfortunate that some parents won't take their adolescent child to a mental health professional if their child doesn't want to go. Taking your child to a mental health professional is no different than taking your child to a dentist for an abscessed tooth or taking your child to a physician for a broken arm. Your child may not want to go to the dentist or to the physician, but you take him or her anyway because that abscessed tooth or broken arm needs to be dealt with immediately. Likewise, when your child has emotional and psychological needs, those needs should be dealt with immediately.

In situations where your child is resistant to visiting with a mental health professional, you merely play the role of a Borg in a Star Trek episode and state the following to your child, "Resistance is futile! You will be assimilated!" In other words, you are the parent and your child is going to do what you want them to do. In some cases, I encourage parents to dangle a major consequence if their child does not comply, along with dangling a big reward if they do comply.

7. *Neuropsychological Impairment.*

Unfortunately, due to the alignment of the planets, the luck of the draw, the effects of general sin on mankind when Adam and Eve fell in the Garden of Eden, or the abuse of alcohol and drugs by a pregnant mother, some children are born with neuropsychological impairment. It seems like every book I read has a computer analogy to explain an author's point of view, so I might as well give it a shot too.

Someone having a chemical imbalance in their brain that causes depression is equivalent to a computer with a software problem. Software problems can be corrected by reconfiguring the data, by simply deleting the software from the hard drive and getting a new disc, or by reinstalling the desired software again. The bottom line is, software problems can be corrected. However, hard drive problems cannot be reconfigured. If your modem goes belly up, it is history. It is time to get a new modem. When parts of our brain go belly up, they can't be replaced. Therefore, neuropsychological impairment tends to be a lifelong problem.

However, I have a very good psychologist friend who would adamantly argue against the above statement. He told me that he "fried" his brain on numerous illicit drugs when he was younger and that God healed him. Who am I to argue against his life experiences? He's certainly one of the smartest guys I know. If his brain was "fried" in the past, it has definitely been healed based on how he conducts himself today. Sometimes, existing neurons can develop new pathways in the brain to make up for deficiencies. The brain is a marvelously created organ.

If you abused alcohol or other drugs while you were pregnant with your child, you may want to have your child evaluated by a pediatrician, neurologist, or neuropsychologist. Certainly a child with neuropsychological impairment will have difficulty complying with the rules at home and at school. You might have to adjust your expectations to match your child's ability to comply in this unique situation. On the other hand, it's possible that the FAMILY system may be inappropriate for your child's developmental needs. By all means, if you suspect that your child may have some form of neuropsychological impairment, please have an evaluation done immediately.

8. Emotionally Disturbed.

Let's face it, we have some pretty sick puppies living in our society today. Unfortunately, there are many broken homes as the result of many extremely dysfunctional adults. Some children have been raked over the coals of emotional abuse during their short years on this planet. As a result of the emotional abuse, their trust level with anyone on this planet is zilch. More often these children fend for themselves, attempting to meet their own needs because they haven't perceived anyone else meeting their needs. They will do whatever it takes to meet their own perceived emotional needs, even if it means defying adult authority at home and at school. More often than not, these children are found in foster homes, group homes, and in families where multiple divorces have occurred. In these situations, your best bet is to put the FAMILY system on hold and get your child the therapy needed to get his or her emotional feet on the ground. Only implement FAMILY when the child is more emotionally stable.

9. Conduct Disorder.

I am seeing an increase in the number of conduct disordered children entering my office for help. Conduct disordered children have a real strong tendency to violate social norms, rules, and laws in their homes, schools, churches, synagogues, and communities. Conduct disordered children will lie, cheat, steal, use force to get what they want, and ultimately defy any perceived authority. As a matter of fact, they will tell most authority figures in their life to take a long walk on a short pier. When conduct disordered adolescents enter therapy, the odds of them turning their behaviors around without order and structure is next to nothing. Fortunately, FAMILY has been used to turn such children around.

To be honest, it is the teeth that can be found in the FAMILY system that helps some of these children turn their lives around in a positive direction. The teeth that I am referring to is the threat of being sent away to long term residential treatment if they continue to choose to disobey rules at home, school, church, synagogue, and in the community. With a conduct disordered child, you may have to be willing to work through your own guilt in order to get your child the help needed. Please don't forget that reverent fear of authority is good. The potential consequences the authority figure can impose upon a disobedient child can be a very productive motivational tool as long as it's legal, moral, and ethical.

Among some adolescents in Fairbanks, Alaska, I was known as the psychologist who sends kids away. I am now slowly developing this same reputation among adolescents in Grants Pass, Oregon. One evening, while standing in line at a video store in Fairbanks, a group of adolescent boys were whispering to one another and looking over their shoulders at me and whispering again. They left the store quickly. The young man behind the counter stated, "What is this 'Dr. J.' stuff? Why are they talking about you sending kids away?" I responded to the young man by saying, "I don't send kids away. Kids make the decision to send themselves away by disobeying their parents and school authorities. Besides, no kid is ever sent away without parental consent."

Recently, I had a parent call me up and ask, "Are you the psychologist who sends kids away? I want you to help me send my kid to long-term residential treatment right now." I responded by saying, "Hold on. Let's get together to talk about why you think your child needs to be sent away. Sending a child away to long-term residential treatment is a last resort option. I want to make sure we have tried everything else first. My goal is to turn your child around so that he or she can remain in your home." The moral of the story is this: don't be so quick to want to send your child away. Besides, residential treatment costs a lot more money than your local outpatient counselor does.

10. Undisclosed Abuse(s).

While providing therapy, it saddens me to discover that a child or adolescent has been physically or sexually abused by a family member, baby sitter, extended family member, or stranger. Obviously, a child that has been sexually abused and chooses to consciously or unconsciously suppress the memory, finds it difficult to trust an authority figure.

There is a lot of controversy out there among mental health professionals concerning repressed memories. I really hesitate to go digging for repressed memories. The bottom line for now is research studies are showing that the retrieval of repressed memories via hypnosis is unreliable. Memory reconstruction can occur and events can be recalled that don't fit with reality. My belief is that memories will surface if the person is psychologically prepared to deal with them. I greatly discourage the use of hypnotherapy to retrieve memories because of it's unreliability. There are many variables involved such as how questions are asked, what someone wants to believe happened, or what someone doesn't want to believe happened. Hypnotherapy is useful for other forms of psychotherapeutic treatment such as for the suppression of nicotine cravings or to help an athlete focus better during competition; however, as previously mentioned, hypnotherapy has not proven itself completely reliable concerning memory retrieval.

When I began my course work at Rutgers University in New Jersey to obtain my Master of Social Work degree, I was told that the best way to be a good therapist was to go through therapy myself. It was important as a clinician to know what it was like to be in the client's chair. Fortunately, Rutgers University provided free counseling for graduate students. I knew I had to deal with a lot of anger, grief, and loss issues in therapy. Therefore, I was more than happy to take advantage of the free counseling. I spent a year in therapy with a wonderful psychologist, who helped me to deal with many of my unresolved family issues from childhood.

During my year of individual therapy, I did not inform my psychologist about something that began years before. Since the age of nine, I had been having the same dream over and over again. The dream always started with me being a young boy sitting on the couch in my parents' home. I was home alone. It was dark outside and only the living room lights were on. Then as usual, in my dream, I would hear a noise upstairs in the large bedroom attic. The door at the bottom of the stairs would open up with a creaking sound. In my dream, as that young boy, I would be sitting on the couch shaking with fear as I watched the door open up to the living room. It was at that point in my dream that I would always wake up still shaking with fear.

For the first time in 18 years, while primarily addressing my anger toward my parents as well as some grief and loss issues concerning a past relationship in my life, my dream began to progress beyond just sitting scared on the couch. There I was, a little boy, all alone, sitting on the couch again. Something was banging around upstairs and making noise in the large attic bedroom. The door at the bottom of the stairs creaked as it opened up. This time, I got up off the couch and nervously walked over to the door and opened it up. Then I woke up from my dream with overwhelming fear and trembling. In the next dream, on a different night, I made it to the bottom of the stairs and tried to turn on the light, only to be left standing in darkness. I woke up with fear and trembling again.

In the next phase of the dream, I made it to the top of the stairs in the dark and tried to turn on the light without success. I woke up again with fear and trembling. In the next phase of the dream on a different night, I made my way up the stairs and down to the end of the attic bedroom in the pitch dark and tried to turn on the light without success. I woke up again with overwhelming fear and trembling. As an adult male, I found it hard to deal with feeling like a helpless little child. I couldn't talk with my psychologist or my wife about my dreams. I was too embarrassed. Hurrah for the macho male ego!

Finally, toward the end of my year of individual therapy at Rutgers University, my dream progressed to a climax. During the last time I ever had that dream, I was an adult sitting on the couch in my parents' house, home alone. I was no longer the scared little boy. I heard the noise upstairs and began to breathe heavily with rage. Seriously, I probably sounded like a woman in labor breathing fast and hard while experiencing contractions. I ran over to the door at the bottom of the stairs, jerked it open, and did not bother to turn on the light switch. I ran up to the top of the stairs, into the dark attic bedroom, more enraged than ever. I made my way to the other end of the dark attic bedroom. I was flailing my arms in the dark trying to find whatever it was that had been making that noise all those years in my dreams. When I found it in the dark, I was going to kill it with every ounce of rage that my body and soul could muster.

While I was experiencing this climatic dream, my wife awoke because of my heavy breathing. She knew something was wrong because normally I am a very quiet sleeper. I seldom ever snore. She decided to wake me up from my obvious nightmare. She grabbed my wrist and began shaking it in order to wake me up.

Meanwhile, back to my climatic dream. I had reached the last spot in that large pitch black attic bedroom and whatever I was looking for grabbed my wrist. It's Murphy's Law to find what your looking for in the last place you look. In my dream, I grabbed whatever it was, took it's hand off my wrist, clenched my other hand into a fist, and pulled my arm back to give this tormentor of mine the most powerful and deadly blow I could deliver. The heavy weight champion boxer of the world could not withstand this wrathful blow.

Meanwhile, back in the waking world, my wife began to scream my name, "Matt! Matt!" She was legitimately concerned that I was about to hit her. While sleeping, I had grabbed her wrist with my left hand, pulled her hand off my wrist and had cocked my right arm. Fortunately for Rochelle, her screaming my name woke me up before I decked whatever it was in my dream - and her. I immediately experienced a memory flashback.

For a brief moment, I saw something like a movie on a motion picture screen. The spot in the upstairs attic in my dream, where the thing grabbed my wrist in the dark, was the exact spot where an older adolescent male sexually abused me when I was nine years old. He was about six years older than me. I looked up to him. I trusted him. All the pain and anger came flowing out of me right there in my bed. My repressed memories were freed when I was emotionally and psychologically prepared to deal with them. I did not need hypnotherapy to accomplish this end result.

At my last therapy session, I informed my psychologist about the dream and it's progression during my year of therapy. She believed that my addressing the dysfunctional family issues I grew up with on a conscious level, freed me up to face issues of sexual abuse in my dreams at an unconscious level. For 18 years I had stuffed the pain and anger of the betrayal I had experienced at the hand of my older adolescent male friend, whom I admired and trusted.

I can personally testify to the fact that my angry distrust toward authority figures pretty much diminished because of my own issues surfaced when I was emotionally and psychologically prepared to deal with them. Never underestimate the power of the mind, especially the unconscious mind, and how it impacts the choices made by a child or an adult. If you suspect that your child has experienced undisclosed abuses, once again, please seek the assistance of a licensed mental health professional. Insist that the therapist doesn't try to force the issue to surface before your child is actually ready to face it. Your child's mind will allow him or her to process their issues when they are prepared to do so. In other words, you might have to wait until your child becomes an adult.

Part 2
The Mechanics of
the FAMILY System

8   *The FAMILY System*

THIS IS THE LONGEST and most important chapter of the book. However, before you read this chapter, you really need to read and understand the first seven chapters. Have you read the first seven chapters yet? Yes, you! I'm writing to you! You know who you are! That's right! The individual who likes to skip ahead rather than take the time to read a book in it's proper order. Well, aren't you special! The nuts and bolts of FAMILY will not make absolute sense to you unless you first read chapters one through seven. So stop reading this chapter and start at the beginning of the book just like everyone else does. Hey! I said stop! A thorough understanding of the philosophical underpinnings of FAMILY is essential to making complete and absolute sense out of the nuts and bolts of the FAMILY system. Okay, I'll catch up with you later after you enlighten yourself. I know. Life is difficult when you are sequentially impaired. You'll survive! Trust me! Go back to chapter one right this second. I'll see you back here in chapter eight in a little while. Bye!

For those of you who have actually read the first seven chapters, I wish to explain the ultimate goal of FAMILY. The ultimate goal of FAMILY is not to create perfect parents and children. Rather, the ultimate goal of FAMILY is to improve communication in the home through clarification of the rules, consequences, and rewards. This process will eventually lead to less tension and conflict among family members and ultimately lead to more compliant and respectful behaviors from everyone toward everyone.

It is my most humble opinion that all families in America should be federally mandated to implement FAMILY in their homes. Most problems in our society can be traced to the home and the lack of organized and structured discipline parents are providing for their children. As much as they might rebel and protest, children and adolescents want their parents to provide structure and guidance. They want to know that their parents are committed to keeping them safe and on the right path in life.

Although children have free will and can therefore make unhealthy choices, the provision of organized structure and clarified communication will help to significantly reduce the likelihood that they will make inappropriate choices. This is the ultimate goal of FAMILY: To assist families via improved communication, learning to make appropriate choices, and taking responsibility for their actions. If you make a mistake while implementing FAMILY in your home, admit it, get back up on the horse and keep riding. Don't quit because you are struggling with being consistent. Work on becoming more consistent. FAMILY works if you work it! (Please see Appendix B for FAMILY testimonials).

Before you implement the FAMILY system in your home, you will need the following materials:

1. Paper and pen or a computer and printer. You will be recording your parental expectations on paper. Hint: The age of computers is upon us and using a computer makes it a whole lot easier to add to the list, delete from the list, or modify the existing list of family rules.

2. A minimum of 55 (3 x 5) index cards which will be used for your Good Habit cards, Wild Cards, and Grace Cards.

3. A whole bunch of different colored poker chips or other similar items to be used as FAMILY tokens and RAK chips.

4. A very serious commitment to the Correct and Consistent implementation of FAMILY in your home (i.e., "the two 'C' words"). For the sake of beating a dead horse, "correct" means implementing the system the way I teach it to you in this book – no deviations. Please remember, I've taught this to several thousand families. I have taught FAMILY to licensed mental health

professionals. They have given me truckloads of feedback. We've already been there, done that, and got the T-shirt. What you're reading is what has been proven to work the best. So don't try and create a hybrid of FAMILY. You may think your family is uniquely different, but it's not. We are all a lot more alike than most of us would care to admit. The kinks of FAMILY have been worked out. "Consistent" means keep your parenting roles properly prioritized and "keep on keeping on." This means implementing FAMILY in spite of your changing moods or energy levels. Finally, keep on consistently implementing FAMILY in your home especially when behaviors are going smoothly. Don't forget. Take FAMILY until it's all gone – until your last child is eighteen, graduated from high school, and moved out of the home. Then you can go back to being an unstructured and unorganized slob if you so desire.

Please remember, "Every family needs a FAMILY." Now, without further adieu, it is a pleasure for me to introduce FAMILY to you!

Fashion a List of Family Rules

1. Nothing goes on the list of family rules unless both parents are in agreement (i.e., Both parents have equal veto power). I encourage cooperation and not a power struggle. If you can't work together on something this simple, then you definitely need marital counseling before you implement FAMILY. If you are a single parent, you can attempt to consult with your ex-spouse, in order to implement FAMILY in both homes. If your former spouse is deceased, out of contact with the family, or uncooperative, then seek input from an adult friend.

2. The list of rules are to govern behaviors for all family members at home, school, work, malls, church, synagogue, 30,000 feet up in the air in a jet, 2,000 feet below the surface of the ocean in a submarine, and everywhere else in between.

3. The rules are to be "Do as we say and as we do" rules. Parents are expected to practice what they preach. If you don't want your kids to swear, then you don't swear. If you want your

kids to make their bed in the morning then you make your bed in the morning. The only exceptions are issues of legal age (e.g., Driving, drinking, smoking, movies, curfew, etc.) and maturity (e.g., Bedtime, phone time, etc.). Note: Dr. J. encourages parents not to drink and smoke.

4. Parents may seek input from their child(ren) concerning what rules to put on the list but parents always have the final say (i.e., Authority flows downward). Remember, you are a benevolent dictator. If your child(ren) think(s) they are in control of the family, they may engage you in a power struggle in an attempt to maintain their perceived control. More often than not, it is best not to consult with your children, especially if they are oppositional. God didn't consult with humanity before giving us the 10 commandments. Rather, God gave us the 10 commandments - not the 10 suggestions.

5. Rules can be added to, deleted from, or modified on the list at anytime as long as the parents talk with each other first and are both in agreement. Remember this is a flexible, living, and breathing document. It is never chiseled into stone - FAMILY is not rigid. FAMILY can change with the needs of the moment and the developmental changes in your children.

6. If the rule is not on the list, then it is not a rule and your child(ren) did not break it. It would not be right if a State Trooper attempted to arrest you because he or she did not like the glasses you were wearing or the color of your hair. There is no state law telling us what kind of glasses we can and cannot wear nor is there a state law telling us what color of hair we can and cannot have. Therefore, you better thoroughly think through what rules you want to put on the family list and whether or not you are prepared to enforce them both correctly and consistently. (See Appendix C for a sample of the most commonly used family rules).

7. You cannot create a new rule and retroactively go back and nail your child(ren) for breaking it. Your children must be informed first about any additions or modifications to the house rules list before they can be held accountable for breaking the rule(s).

8. On the average, most parents come up with approximately 35 rules. I have seen as few as 5 rules and as many as 50 rules. Please number the family rules for easy reference at a later time. Professionals who recommend a limited number of rules in a home are from another planet and have obviously never parented your children before. In the real world, we live by more than 10 total rules and we all manage to cope just fine without feeling overwhelmed or having our self-esteem shattered.

9. I will not tell you what rules you should use to raise your children. FAMILY is the skeletal framework of organization and you get to slap on the meat and skin in a manner that reflects your values and morals. All parents need to work through what values and morals they want to teach their children. Every home is different; however, it is not uncommon for parents to want feedback from other parents or professionals to see if they are being too lenient or too rigid with their list of family rules. I am available for consultation at drj@family-rules.com (Please see Appendix C or consult with an adult friend whose parenting abilities you respect). You may also look at my web page, to see if there is a "FAMILY Rules Counselor" in your community (www.family-rules.com). Ultimately, you have to make the final decision on what rules you need to have to raise your children.

Fashion a List of Family Rules
Add Good Habit Cards

1. Take forty-five 3x5 index cards and write various "good habits" on them that last approximately $1/2$ hour in length — give or take 10-minutes (e.g., sweep and mop the kitchen floor, clean the toilet and bathtub, clean out the inside of mom's car, bake a cake, write a letter to grandma, 50 jumping jacks/50 sit-ups, read a book to your younger sibling, etc.). You may create separate stacks of cards for older and younger children. (Please see Appendix D).

2. The good habit cards are to consist of tasks above and beyond your child(ren)'s daily and weekly chores (i.e., daily and weekly chores do not go on the good habit cards).

3. You may wish to designate some cards as seasonal cards (for example, five yellow cards for outdoor summer tasks and 5 blue cards for outdoor winter tasks), or you may wish to divide one card with a diagonal slash and write "shovel drive way in winter/sweep drive way in summer."

4. Take five 3x5 index cards and simply write "Wild Card" on them. This means that your child(ren) has to do whatever you want them to do for approximately 30-minutes. Also, when you pull a "Wild Card," you have to do whatever your children want you to do for approximately 30 minutes. This teaches family members the principle of "what goes around comes around" or "do unto others as you would have them do unto you." In other words, my family members usually pick interactive tasks such as playing catch or board games or going for a bike ride. You now have a total of 50 good habit cards.

5. Take an additional five 3x5 index cards and write "Grace" on them. If your child draws this card, they are off the hook for this particular card. They get some "amazing grace, how sweet the sound that saved a wretch like" them. You now have a total of 55 cards.

6. Assign good habit card values within the parentheses in the left margin of the page next to the numbered list of family rules (Please see Appendix C). Start low and work your way up from there (i.e., 1-3 cards); however, start with a high number of Good Habit cards for the most important rules. Most parents put 50 cards next to "Obey all local, state, federal, and military laws."

Fashion a List of Family Rules
Add Good Habit Cards
Mix in Responsibility via Household Chores

1. Develop a list of daily chores. Daily chores need to have inspection times (for example, feed and water the dog before dinner; brush your teeth before school and before bed; etc.). (Please see Appendix E).

2. Develop a list of weekly chores. Weekly chores need to have an inspection day and time (e.g., clean and vacuum your bedroom by 12:00 P.M. on Saturday). Note: Do not set an inspection time at a time when you cannot inspect it. If you don't get home until 5:30 P.M., don't set the inspection time at 4:30 P.M. Instead, set it at 6:00 P.M.

3. Parents, you don't need to nag your child(ren) anymore about completing their chores. You just simply check them out at the inspection time and render a verdict. If the child didn't complete the chore(s) on time, they will receive a good habit card per unfinished chore and they will need to complete their chore(s) immediately.

4. Parents, don't forget to make up your own list of daily and weekly chores. Yes! I know you already do plenty around the house. Writing down the daily and weekly tasks you do around the house allows your children to notice all that you do. Don't assume that they are completely aware of your contributions to the household. Also, wives, FAMILY provides you with the wonderful opportunity to create a daily and weekly "Honey Do" list for your hubby. He will appreciate it. Spread your work load out and stop being a domestic martyr! Finally, I don't want to hear, "But no one does it as good or neat as I do." If your kids are slobs, then teach them to do it right. Otherwise, you are enabling them to be slobs.

How "F" & "A" & "M" Work Together

1. When FAMILY is officially implemented, parents will no longer be in charge of whether or not their children are grounded nor will they be in charge of how long their children are grounded. Instead, their children will be in charge of whether or not they are grounded and for how long they are grounded. They will learn to take responsibility for their choices.

2. If children break a rule or do not do their daily or weekly chores, they are choosing to ground themselves. Parents never ask children to break rules — children choose to break rules.

3. When children choose to break a rule, they will need to randomly select the assigned number of good habit cards from the top of the deck without looking at what they are drawing. The number of good habit cards will have been previously designated by parents and placed in parenthesis next to each rule on the family rules list. The more significant the rule, the more good habit cards they will receive for breaking it (Please see Appendix C).

4. The child(ren) must accept their good habit cards politely or they will be doubled each time they are inappropriate, so that 2 cards become 4; 4 cards double to 8 cards; 8 cards double to 16 cards; 16 cards double to 32 cards; and 32 cards max out at 50. Children feel like they are in a hole they can't climb out of if given more than 50 cards. Give your child a "ten minute cooling down period" in between doubling the cards for impoliteness. This will give both the child and you an opportunity to calm down and hopefully contribute toward de-escalating the situation. If you find yourself losing control of your temper, calm down first and then discipline. You will be much more effective in the long run.

5. After a child draws a card (or cards), he or she has two choices:

   A. Do the good habit card(s) immediately, or
   B. Go to his or her room and do the good habit card(s) later. With this option, the child is merely choosing to lengthen the grounding. The choice belongs to the child and not to the parents.

6. After a child completes the instructions on the cards, he or she is required to have their parent(s) inspect the job to see if it was done correctly. If not done correctly, errors are politely pointed out and the child is asked to finish the job. Parents might have to show a younger child what is expected by helping with the chore. Once the good habit card is completed correctly, it is returned to the discard pile and parents do not mention the offense again. After a child has "done the time for the crime," parents should cast their child's sins "as far as the east is from the west and remember those

sins no more." However, if the chore is inspected for a second time and it's obvious that no effort was put into completing the chore correctly, even after giving specific instructions, then the child selects another good habit card. Have him or her complete the present task before moving on to the next one.

7. If the child chooses to go to his or her room, he or she may only do four things while in the room:

    A. They can lay on the bed (this includes taking a nap)
    B. Do their homework
    C. Engage in parent approved reading
    D. Clean the room.

The child cannot do anything else. No TV, no stereo, no computer, no phone, no toys, no puzzles, nothing but the above mentioned activities (which usually is perceived as absolute and total boredom). Bummer! If the child doesn't cooperate, see how to respond under "Y" on page 110.

8 If the child chooses to go to his or her room, there are only seven reasons for leaving the room:

    A. To go to the bathroom for a brief period of time
    B. To eat a family meal
    C. To go to school or participate in a school activity (drama, band, sports, etc.)
    D. To go to work if he or she has a shift job
    E. To go to church/synagogue (regular worship service and Sunday school only)
    F. To go to a 12-step meeting
    G. To complete the good habit card(s) if it is not past their bedtime. If it is past his or her bed time, then the card(s) carry over to the next day.

Note: Most children who choose to go to their room, only stay there for 10 to 30 minutes. They just want space and time to calm down. Leave them alone unless they are destroying their room. If they are destroying their room, remind them about "strikes" and "pop flies."

9. If parents break a rule, they will need to do the assigned good habit card(s) immediately. The best parenting technique on planet earth is consistent role modeling (i.e., practice what you preach and walk the talk). "Do as we say and not as we do" is unacceptable. We all make mistakes from time to time; however, to knowingly practice hypocrisy is a major parenting mistake. If you make a mistake, admit it, do your cards, and keep on parenting.

10. If a parent should ever refuse to do his or her card(s), children have the right to bring this issue to the attention of the other parent or mutually accepted adult mediator. The parents will have a private discussion. If the fallen parent emerges from the bedroom with a spirit of repentance and does the card(s), then the dilemma is considered resolved; however, if the fallen parent does not repent, then the rule that was broken is temporarily suspended until the offending parent gets his or her card(s) done. For example, if the parent cussed and refuses to do the good habit card, even after the other parent or adult mediator talks with him or her, then the "no cussing" rule is temporarily suspended and the children may cuss all they want until the parent completes the card(s). In other words, walk the talk and practice what you preach. Please don't be a practicing hypocrite!

We are all hypocrites. No one is perfect. We all break the rules from time to time and/or occasionally violate our personal/ spiritual morals, values and ethics. Hopefully, this doesn't happen very often. FAMILY does not expect parents to be perfect; however, FAMILY does expect parents to try and be the best role models they can be for their children. We need to strive to better our character and conduct on a daily basis. If you make a mistake, admit it and do your cards immediately, and keep on parenting. It's one thing to make mistakes or to occasionally and unintentionally break the rules. However, it's another thing to intentionally break the rules on a continuous basis without remorse or repentance. Knowingly and intentionally practicing ongoing hypocrisy is unacceptable and outright lousy parenting. Matter of fact, it's reprehensible and impeachable! Go to bed every night knowing you were a better parent than the day before. Always strive to be better. Strive for excellence even if you make mistakes along the journey of parenting. Don't settle for mediocrity. Your children are watching you. Monkey see, monkey do. The acorn doesn't fall too far from the tree. They're a chip off the old block.

Fashion a List of Family Rules
Add Good Habit Cards
Mix in Responsibility via Household Chores
Institute a List of Rewards

1. Sit down with your child(ren) and develop a list of rewards that meet with your approval and fit within your financial realities. I have seen a variety of rewards offered by parents: ice cream cones, video rentals, slumber parties, movies with a friend (popcorn and soda provided), shoes, CD's, clothes, fishing trips, concerts, shopping sprees, and many more items. Please number the rewards list for easy reference in the future (Please see Appendix F).

2. Once you have developed the list of rewards and numbered them, assign a FAMILY token value for each reward. Rule of thumb: The bigger and better the reward, the more tokens it will cost your child(ren). (Please see appendix F).

3. Most parents place a minimum value of $ 1.00 per FAMILY token. Sometimes, parents will choose to lower the number of FAMILY tokens required to obtain a bigger and better reward to give their child(ren) extra incentive to obtain the desired reward (e.g., a $ 100.00 pair of designer tennis shoes will be offered for 75 tokens rather than 100 tokens).

4. Your children earn FAMILY tokens as follows: Every night, at bedtime, you consistently and quickly recall the day to deter-

mine how your child(ren) behaved. If they didn't break a rule and they got all of their chores done, then they receive a FAMILY token. If they broke a rule and/or didn't get their chore(s) done, then they don't receive a FAMILY token. Sorry parents, you don't get FAMILY tokens. Peace and quiet via improved communication and increased compliance with the rules of your home is reward enough for most parents.

5. Each child has his or her own color coded tokens (poker chips) to discourage stealing. Yes, your kids would actually rip each other off, so plan ahead and prevent it from happening.

6. If your children receive all 7 FAMILY tokens for the week (Sunday through Saturday), they will receive three bonus FAMILY tokens. Therefore, they will receive a total of 10 FAMILY tokens for a perfect week. Use a calendar to help you keep track of this.

7. If your children receive FAMILY tokens from the first day of the month through the last day of the month, they will not only receive 10 FAMILY tokens x 4 weeks (equaling a total of 40 FAMILY tokens), they will also receive 10 bonus tokens for a perfect month (equaling a total of 50 FAMILY tokens for the month). Don't forget to use a calendar.

A Side Note Concerning Allowance for Children

Some child psychologists believe that children should receive an allowance no matter how good or bad they have behaved (i.e., allowance should not be tied in with their behaviors). Instead, the allowance should be used as a teaching tool to help children learn how to manage their money. Most parents give their children a set amount on a weekly basis and then teach them to save 20%, give 10% to a local charity, church or synagogue (i.e., teaching them to give back to their community), and do whatever they want with the remaining 70%. The amount you choose to give your children for their weekly allowance depends upon your financial realities. If you attempt to tie in their allowance with behaviors, then it interferes with your ability to teach them how to manage their money appropriately. Their behaviors will be dealt with sufficiently via the good habit cards and tokens. Don't forget to correctly and consistently implement FAMILY in your home (the two "C" words).

Fashion a List of Family Rules
Add Good Habit Cards
Mix in Responsibility via Household Chores
Institute a List of Rewards
Love and Encourage Your Child(ren) Daily

1. You can never overstate the fact to your child(ren) that you love them. Compliment and praise your children daily. Give them hugs and kisses. Tell them that they look nice. Let them know that you love them unconditionally. Brag about them to your friends. Don't worry if they think it's uncool. Deep down inside, they appreciate the positive attention. They really do! Really!

2. If you catch your child(ren) engaged in Random Acts of Kindness, give them a RAK chip. This RAK chip obviously needs to be a different color than all of the other FAMILY tokens. Three RAK chips equal one regular FAMILY token. This way there is still incentive for your child(ren) to behave appropriately during the course of a day, even if they have already broken a rule and/or failed to complete their chore(s). They can exchange RAK chips for FAMILY tokens and still have a chance to make a perfect week and/or month (kind of like extra credit).

3. Even though there is an opportunity for your child(ren) to earn rewards, this should not stop you from occasionally spoiling them rotten just for the fun of it. You can still take them out to dinner or buy them a gift just because they are special and have been behaving well.

4. Provide your child(ren) with opportunities to tell you how

they think and feel about what is going on in the home. They must be respectful. Spend one on one time with them. I try the best I can to take my kids out for breakfast every now and then. This provides them with a consistent opportunity to talk about anything they want to or need to with dad.

5. Schedule a weekly family meeting. Place a family journal in a central location so that everyone in the family has an opportunity to write down what they want to discuss at the next family meeting. If it is not written down at least one-hour prior to the meeting, then it will not be discussed. It will have to wait until next week. Everyone needs to know what will be discussed so there are no surprises. Discuss old business first and then new business. Positive things may be discussed. This is not meant to just be a gripe session. Meeting length varies.

Fashion a List of Family Rules
Add Good Habit Cards
Mix in Responsibility via Household Chores
Institute a List of Rewards
Love and Encourage Your Child(ren) Daily
Youth Residential Treatment if Needed

1. Rules without teeth are not worth the paper on which they are written. There must be immediate and consistent consequences for inappropriate behaviors. Otherwise, your children will run your home and chaos will rule (i.e., "He who spares the rod [discipline] hates his child").

2. If your children should ever reach the point where they totally and wholeheartedly defy your authority, they will have committed "strike-one" and they will be automatically grounded to their room for a week. They will miss weekend and extra cur-

ricular activities at school. They will also not be allowed to work their shift job. If they end up being kicked off the team for missing practices and games or being fired from their job for not showing up to work, tough luck! They shouldn't have defied your authority. It's the price they pay for outright disobedience. Upon completion of the one week of grounding to their room, they will have all 50 good habit cards to do.

3. If your children should ever reach the point where they totally and wholeheartedly defy your authority for a second time, they will have committed "strike-two" and they will be automatically grounded to their room for two weeks. Upon completion of the two weeks, they will have all 50 good habit cards to do.

4. If your children should ever reach the point where they totally and wholeheartedly defy your authority for a third time, they will have committed "strike-three" and it will be time for you to pull out the nukes: long-term residential treatment. If you have a child that is out of control, long-term residential treatment is your best option to help modify his or her behaviors (Please see appendix G). Don't forget to search the Internet, family magazines, or inquire at your church or synagogue.

5. There is a difference between a "strike" and a "bad-hair day." A "strike" is total and wholehearted defiance toward your authority. Defiance can be seen in a child's eyes and body language. Most importantly, you can see the total and wholehearted defiance in a child's actions (for example, dropping out of school, continuing to drink and do drugs, involvement in criminal activities, blowing out of therapy, having sex, etc.). A "bad-hair day" will involve some defiance and willfulness but ultimately, your child submits to your authority, takes his or her cards and does them. Absolutely do not give a "strike" to your child because they are having a "bad-hair day." Consult with an objective third party before handing out a "strike."

6. In addition to "strikes," there is such a thing as a "pop-fly." If your child earns a "pop-fly," the child automatically goes to long-term residential treatment. Don't even bother with "strikes"

when your child earns a "pop-fly." Just send him or her to treatment immediately. A "pop-fly" constitutes behavior that is above and beyond defiance of authority. Running away for several days or weeks, major alcohol and drug use activities, assault, major destruction of property, and criminal activity are behaviors that should result in a "pop fly.".

7. Sending your child(ren) to long-term residential treatment does not mean that you or FAMILY has failed. This is an option within the structure of FAMILY to effectively deal with out of control children. If your child had a heart problem and the physicians in your local community could not treat it, you would not hesitate to send your child to a medical facility in another community. Likewise, with behavioral problems, if your child has failed outpatient therapy and is out of control at home, school, and in your community, then it is time to send your child to the appropriate treatment setting. This is wise parenting regardless of the guilt trips you may put yourself through.

   Please remember, your child has a free-will and makes his or her own decisions. Sending the child to live with a divorced spouse or distant relative is the next best option; however, the new household doesn't provide a therapeutic treatment setting with behavior modification. In most cases, the child's behavior worsens when sent to live with a divorced spouse or relative; however, if you can't or won't pay for residential treatment, then let your child terrorize your ex-spouse for a while. Maybe he or she will then be willing to help you out with the expenses of long term residential treatment. If you search the Internet thoroughly or inquire at your local church or synagogue, you'll eventually find a low cost facility. Maybe your state Medicaid office will assist your child. Look at advertisements in family magazines (*Sunset, Better Homes and Gardens, Focus on the Family*, etc.). Don't roll over and play dead in your own house. Do something about it!

8. The bottom line is your children are going to learn how to obey authority. The question is where do they want to learn to obey? Do they want to learn how to obey at home or do they want to learn how obey a few hundred or thousand miles

away in a long-term residential treatment facility? Most children decide to learn how to obey authority at home. Some children need to go bye-bye to learn how to obey authority. Ultimately, the choice to go or stay is up to how your child chooses to comply with your authority in your home.

9. Finally, the money you spend to send your child to a high quality long-term residential treatment facility is a worthwhile investment. The odds are very good that he or she will return home a changed individual with the learned ability to make more positive choices for themselves. But wait a minute, look beyond the fact that you are investing only in your child's future. In reality, if you are helping your child to be a better human-being, then ultimately, you are investing in your grandchildren's future as well. Can you imagine what kind of parent your out of control child will make someday if you don't deal with their destructive behavior here and now? Invest in your child's life and in the lives of your descendants. This is your parental responsibility and an awesome one at that. Go to your grave knowing you did absolutely everything you could for your children and your descendants. You can't take your money with you when you die. Invest your time and money wisely in the things that matter the most - your family. Meet your Maker with a clear conscience. Rest in peace!

9 *Introducing FAMILY In Your Home*

How you present FAMILY to your children and adolescents is very important. The ideal way to explain FAMILY to your children is with the assistance of a therapist who is thoroughly immersed in FAMILY training (i.e., a "FAMILY Rules Counselor"). The "FAMILY Rules Counselor" will be able to offer objectivity to the implementation process. This counselor can also be the "bad guy" if necessary to take the heat off of you. He or she can be available for ongoing monitoring of "correct" and "consistent" implementation of FAMILY in your home if and when needed (i.e., "the two 'C' words"). To see whether or not you have a "FAMILY Rules Counselor" in your community, please contact my website: www.family-rules.com. All "FAMILY Rules Counselor," are posted on my website and have a certificate in their office to verify their training (Please see appendix A).

If you do not have a "FAMILY Rules Counselor" in your area, you may want to encourage your local therapist to contact my private practice office so he or she can make arrangements for becoming a "FAMILY Rules Counselor." Have them call the FAMILY Rules phone number: 1-541-956-8585. They can also learn more about how to become a "FAMILY Rules Counselor" by checking out my website: www.family-rules.com. Remember, your therapist must understand and be fully immersed in the FAMILY system or the odds might significantly increase that he or she may undermine your parental authority and turn your child into a monster. The democratic model of parenting inappropriately empowers children and undermines your parental authority.

The second best way to implement FAMILY in your home is by having your entire family attend a FAMILY seminar in your community. Attending a FAMILY seminar is beneficial for your children because they get to see other families involved in the same endeavor. Many parents lack a reference point for parenting and they often learn just how "normal" they are when they attend a FAMILY seminar. Parents hear other parents expressing concerns about whether or not they are being too strict or too lenient. Parents also get to hear other parents' children asking the presenter the same cute or defiant questions their own children ask at home. A FAMILY seminar provides a place of connection, learning, and encouragement for all family members. To find out more information about how to sponsor a FAMILY seminar at your school, business, civic organization, church, synagogue, or community, please call the FAMILY Rules, Inc. office number: 1-541-956-8585. You may also find out more information about how to sponsor a FAMILY seminar by contacting my website: www.family-rules.com (Please see Appendix I).

The third option, and soon to be the most commonly used method is implementation of FAMILY by parents such as you. Although this approach lacks an objective third party, if everything has been screened concerning unresolved parent issues and children's issues (i.e., please read chapters four through seven), it is very doable.

I have heard many stories through the grapevine regarding how parents and teachers have learned about FAMILY. One evening, while entertaining friends in our home for dinner, we heard one of the stories: The week before, our friends had dinner with a family who had recently met FAMILY. They were pleasantly shocked by the behaviors of this family's children. The kids were sitting well behaved at the table, eating with good manners, and they were not interrupting conversations. If that wasn't surprising enough, this family's children were not bouncing off the walls before and after dinner nor were they arguing or fighting. They were simply playing games and getting along. Can you imagine that? What is this world coming to?!!

I sat at our dining room table with a puzzled look on my face and asked our dinner guests, "What's the point?" They informed me that this family was neither a private practice client of mine nor did they ever attend a FAMILY seminar. The parents knew another family that attended a FAMILY seminar who shared the concepts of FAMILY. As a result, chaos was eliminated from their home and everyone was getting along much better. They were able to do this without the assistance of a professional or by attending a FAMILY seminar. Instead, they got their grubby little hands on my copyrighted materials and used the content for the benefit of their family without paying me a dime. I'm just joking!

I was genuinely pleased to hear about the positive results of FAMILY and how it has helped to improve the home of one more family on this planet. My goal is to work myself out of a job. I seriously don't mind if I get occasional help along the way, but only as long as FAMILY's little elves don't violate copyright laws in the process. Hint! Hint! The mission statement of FAMILY is "Every home needs a FAMILY." My very modest goal is to see FAMILY implemented in every home on this planet. Please help spread the word. Let's restore proper love and respect for God, others, and ourselves in our homes, schools, churches, synagogues, and communities.

Finally, I have taught FAMILY to over 4,000 families. I have also taught FAMILY seminars to parents of public school students in Fairbanks, Alaska; to many churches of different denominations; to licensed clinical social workers at a conference in Anchorage, Alaska; to licensed psychologists and graduate psychology students at a conference in Newberg, Oregon; and to School District "Area C" parents in the greater area of Los Angeles, California. It is a compliment to be asked to do a FAMILY seminar and a blessing to hear the positive feedback from parents at the end of the seminar. You would think I just saved someone's life. Parents leave these seminars and spread the word about FAMILY which helps stabilize even more homes in our world and this gives me great joy.

If you choose to implement FAMILY in your home without the assistance of a "FAMILY Rules Counselor" or without attending one of my FAMILY seminars, then you should proceed as follows (Remember: "correct" and "consistent" implementation is key – "the two 'C' words"):

1. To the best of your ability, make sure that all adults are involved with the development of the list of FAMILY rules (i.e., single parent, married parents, divorced parents who have remarried someone else, etc.). Agreement between all of the adults involved in your child's life helps to promote consistency in your child's world, especially when your child lives in two homes because of a divorce. I have had plenty of ex-spouses work together to develop a list of rules that would apply equally in both homes. Stability was provided for the children and manipulation of the parents was nipped in the bud.

2. Make sure that FAMILY has been edited by all adults involved in the process. Be careful concerning how you word your rules. Your children and adolescents are good little attorneys. They will spot a loophole anywhere and make you pay for it. Remember, your children may be consulted if you so desire, but you have the final say concerning how your home will be run. Authority flows downward. It's best to consult your children about the rules during a family meeting which would occur after you implement FAMILY. Be very careful not to send your children and adolescents a message that they have an equal say in the decision making process in your home. No democratic parenting allowed!

3. Screen all children, adolescents, and adults for possible issues that might interfere with the successful implementation of FAMILY in your home (i.e., psychological testing, medication management needs, counseling needs, etc.). For example, if you have a flaming ADHD child, have him or her tested and treated first before beginning FAMILY. If you have a power struggle going on in your marriage, first get marital counseling and resolve issues that might prevent FAMILY from being successful in your home.

4. Find a safe and neutral environment to meet with the children in order to explain FAMILY to them. Make sure that all adults are present during the explanation process.

5. Identify an adult to be the primary facilitator. This adult should

be the most rational and emotionally controlled adult—one who won't be manipulated by a defiant strong-willed brat. Conduct business and don't loose your cool.

6. Begin with a very relaxed, laid back demeanor. Try to occasionally interject humor when it's appropriate. This approach helps to set a positive tone; however, if you meet outright resistance from one or more of the children, then you become an Alaskan Eagle. Instantly swoop down from the sky with silent grace, grab the little salmon from the river with your talons, and eat it for lunch. Symbolically, of course. No physical abuse or cannibalism allowed. In other words, calmly and swiftly cut to the chase and inform your children about the fact that FAMILY has razor sharp teeth. If they should ever totally defy your authority, then the teeth will be swiftly implemented via a "strike" or "pop fly." The message is "don't push it with the parents."

7. Ask your kids questions about why rules exist. Explain how rules are a part of everyday life no matter where they go on planet earth. Discuss how they already live by rules at home, school, work, church, synagogue, on the road, on airplanes, etc. Ask your children and adolescents how they would feel if there were no more state or federal governments, no more police, no military, no laws, and all the inmates were let out of all the jails and prisons. If you have a smart-mouth child who responds by saying, "No laws. Cool!" Say something like the following back to your smart mouth child: "Oh, I see. It would be cool if Joe Schmoe from down the street came into our home, ripped us off, raped and killed your mom and me in front of the kids, raped you, then tied you and your siblings up, and burned you alive because he decided to set the house on fire? That would be cool?" The smart-mouth child usually understands the need for rules when you help him or her visualize being violated by another human-being. Discuss how rules keep us safe from others and from ourselves.

8. Once your children and adolescents acknowledge the existence and need for rules, explain FAMILY in the correct order: F-A-M; how "F" & "A" & "M" work together; and finally, I-L-Y. In other words, follow the format of chapter eight.

Read chapter eight out loud if necessary. Take time to answer questions along the way. Plan to take one to two hours for this initial explanation process. It's a good idea to read your family rules, out loud, once a week during your family meeting.

9. When you get to "Y," let your children know the difference between "strikes" and simply having a "bad hair day." "Bad hair days" are not strikes. Also, let your children know that the razor sharp teeth clause is a last resort option and that most families never have to send a child to long-term residential treatment. Explain to them that most kids understand FAMILY and will agree to comply because they don't want to be sent away for a year or longer. However, assure them that you will not hesitate to use the teeth FAMILY provides if and when necessary. You will not be a push over. You have a backbone of steel.

10. Give your children from 4 to 7 days to transition into FAMILY before giving out Good Habit cards; however, start giving out FAMILY tokens and RAK chips immediately. Give each child their own copy of the rules, chores, and rewards lists. Post your list of rules on the refrigerator. Inform your children that their friends will be subject to the rules. If their friends break the rules, they do cards just like anyone else in your home. If they refuse to do their cards, send them home. Let them know that they will not be invited back to your home unless they are willing to do their cards for breaking your rules in your home. Talk to their parents before subjecting your child's friends to your family rules.

11. Don't forget your weekly family meetings. You can use part of this time to tweak, tune, adjust and modify FAMILY in your home if and when necessary. Remember, consultation with children is good, but adults have the final say.

12. Walk the talk. Practice what you preach. Do your cards immediately, even if your children didn't see you break the law by driving over the speed limit. You won't believe the powerful, positive effect of parental role-modeling when your children see you consistently tattle on yourself and immediately do your cards without their prodding. Your actions speak louder than your words.

14. The number 13 isn't used in hotels so we won't use it here either. So what if that doesn't make any sense to you. It's my book and I'll write what I want to write. If all else fails, use the FAMILY Rules videos and watch me explain the FAMILY system to your children. There are two FAMILY Rules videos available for purchase: (1) A video explaining to parents how the system works (i.e., for those parents who would rather watch me explain FAMILY to them rather than take the time to read the book), and (2) A humorous video with yours truly explaining the FAMILY Rules system to your children (Grades K-12). You may purchase the FAMILY Rules videos by calling the FAMILY Rules, Inc. office at 1-541-956-8585. You may also order the videos by contacting my website: www.family-rules.com.

Please remember, when you are explaining FAMILY to your children, you are conducting business. The store clerk never yells at the customer on the other side of the counter no matter how rude he or she becomes. Don't undermine your own parental authority by lowering yourself to the position of sibling. If you become emotional, they will have you right where they want you. Don't fall prey to manipulation. Relax and have fun. FAMILY works if you let it. "Every home needs a FAMILY."

10 *Rats And Cockroaches*

No book about parenting discipline systems is complete without discussing rats and cockroaches. After completing my escort of Carl to the residential treatment facility in Western Samoa, I had time to kill on the South Pacific island before I returned home. The next plane wasn't going to leave the island for five days. What a beautiful place to kill time. I met with the staff and took a tour of the long-term residential treatment facility. I spoke with Carl's mother on the phone to inform her about our trip and the transitional time I spent with Carl before dropping him off at the facility.

While killing time in Western Samoa, I decided to hike up a mountain to see Robert Lewis Stevenson's tomb. He was a famous author in the 1800s. When I reached the top of the mountain, soaking wet from the heat and humidity, I was greeted by a couple who hailed from southern California. They were on their honeymoon. We became acquainted via the usual process of exchanging names, professions, height and shoe size (I'm six feet, nine inches tall and I have size sixteen shoes. Almost everyone I meet asks me how tall I am and what size shoes I wear). I learned that they were attorneys. They learned that I was a psychologist. I agreed not to "shrink" them and they agreed not to "sue" me.

Anyway, our conversation quickly turned to the common denominator found in both of our professions - adolescents. We agreed that the 1960s and 1970s (the anti-establishment era) contributed to the decline of the traditional family and the values and morals espoused within the traditional setting. Respect for authority was replaced by questioning authority. Self restraint was replaced by "try everything at least once." Stamina and loyalty during trials and tribulations were replaced by "If the going gets tough, just quit. Try something different." Right and wrong were replaced with "To each his own as long as no one gets hurt" and "Does it work for you or doesn't it work for you?" Well, you get the point.

While sitting on Robert Louis Stevenson's tomb, our conversation progressed. We were amazed by the fact that we were all gainfully employed in our respective professions as the result of the anti-establishment era. Families are breaking apart. Today's adolescents are facing many social pressures and they are a generation without a purpose or cause. These adolescents' parents and peer support groups have failed to pass on the traditional Judeo-Christian values and morals of our society. These traditional morals and values provided social skills and tools to successfully interact with others and to cope with life's many challenges.

Just a little side tangent for a brief moment. It's interesting to see the social movement in America during the past three decades or so. Various American ethnic groups are encouraged by certain elements in our society to learn more about their cultural history and restore the values of their ancestors into their own lives. They are encouraged to learn their native tongues, meals, and religion. All ethnic groups are encouraged to do so except Euro-Americans. Instead, they appear to be encouraged by certain elements in our society to quickly flee their Euro-American/Judeo-Christian roots and cling to the sinking life boat of the popular nebulous virtues of moral relativism. Euro-Americans are being strongly encouraged to believe in anything they want to believe in, but not to cling to Judeo-Christian values like their forefathers did. Stop believing in right and wrong. Trust the wisdom of the opinion polls and your heart. Following the will of the people is now more important than obeying the rule of law. Euro-Americans are encouraged to believe in any god they want to believe in, but they are strongly discouraged from believing in their Euro-American concept of the Judeo-Christian God; however, that's another book to be written in the future. Thank you for humoring me. Now, back to our story.

As a result of the anti-establishment era, all three of us were gainfully employed. One of us picks up Humpty Dumpty's broken pieces due to his falling off the wall, another prosecutes Humpty Dumpty for falling off the wall, and another defends Humpty Dumpty's right to fall off the wall and to break into little pieces. We all agreed that we would rather have healthy families in our society and be forced to work in different professions; however, this probably won't happen in our lifetime. Unfortunately, I have job security.

Then our conversation took a turn for the worse. The prosecuting attorney talked about "the rats breeding behind the walls." With a puzzled look on my face, I asked for clarification, "What do you mean by rats breeding behind the walls?" Having lived in Alaska in the past, I had difficulty visualizing anything but ice behind the walls. He proceeded to discuss his fears about the problems our society will be facing in one or two more decades when this present generation produces the next generation of adolescents. In other words, the rats are breeding behind the walls. We concluded that there is a growing chasm in our society between those children who are being raised with respect and love for God, others, and self, versus those children who are being raised with a self-centered, victimized, sociopathic, defiant, godless existence. Unless things change quickly, we had better start building the walls around New York City and Los Angeles because the "Escape From" movies will soon become a reality. Just watch the videos, "Escape from New York City" or "Escape from Los Angeles" and you'll get the picture. Please don't let your kids watch these videos!

The rats are breeding behind the walls and the only thing we can do about it is to help one family at a time. This is where you come into play. Yes, you! The reader of this book. You have the responsibility of analyzing where you are at individually, as a spouse, if married, and as a parent. Are you honestly and seriously facing your issues? Are you receiving therapeutic, medical, and/or spiritual help as needed? How are you raising your children? Are you stressed out, tired, rolling over and playing dead while your children run the home and aimlessly run the streets? Do you have support and encouragement from a parents' group, 12-Step group, synagogue, or local church? Are you fulfilling the responsibility of proactively raising your children or are you hoping they'll grow up quickly and leave the home sooner than later? You can help nip tomorrow's problems in the bud by proactively raising your children today. I hope and pray you are not contributing to the breeding of the rats behind the walls.

Now let us contemplate cockroaches in the kitchen, which is another matter I have difficulty visualizing, having lived in Alaska in the past. A black bear in the kitchen? Yes. Cockroaches in the kitchen? No. Thank the Lord it is too cold in Alaska for cockroaches to thrive. Give me a grizzly bear or moose any day! We don't have cockroaches in our home in Grants Pass, Oregon either. Whew!

When you implement FAMILY in your home, it will be like turning on the kitchen light at midnight in a Florida home. The cockroaches in the kitchen will scurry. They'll run for cover. They don't want to be seen. Likewise, FAMILY will shed the true light on every member of the home and what role they play in the familial dysfunction. Is dad or mom over controlling and unwilling to share power? Are the adults parenting the children or are the children parenting the adults? Who tends to make up excuses and not take responsibility for their choices? Do one or both adults in the home walk the talk by practicing what they preach? Just how genuinely compliant or defiant are your children to your authority?

Rick and Delores attended a FAMILY seminar with their son, Frank. Afterwards, they contacted me to set up counseling sessions for their family. Rick and Delores were experiencing difficulty with the successful implementation of FAMILY because Frank was being a good little attorney. He was finding loopholes and splitting hairs. In other words, he was being passive-aggressive toward his parents and the spirit of the law. Truth and genuine compliance was not at the forefront of Frank's mind.

As we upped the ante in therapy via FAMILY consequences, Frank's absolute defiance became more and more clear to Rick and Delores. This was difficult for them to see and accept. Rick and Delores became nosy and found out that Frank had downloaded pornography from the Internet. He had also obtained information on how to make bombs. He had obtained a private mailbox in order to receive inappropriate letters. Finally, Frank obtained an online server and paid for it with the money he made while working at a fast food restaurant. Rick and Delores had no idea that Frank was doing all this stuff behind their backs. After all, they had canceled their local online server. Isn't it amazing what services our children can obtain without parental permission? The businesses didn't even try to contact Rick and Delores to see if it was okay with them. Talk about civil-suit possibilities!

In Rick and Delores' situation, FAMILY clearly shed the light on where Frank's frame of mind was. As a result, Rick and Delores chose to send Frank to a long-term residential treatment facility in Montana. Frank is slowly making progress on his issues. He's learning to take responsibility for his inappropriate choices. Frank is beginning to face life in an honest manner. Obviously, Rick and Delores are ecstatic about Frank's progress and can't wait to have him come back home.

Another situation where the impact of FAMILY clearly shed light on a family's dysfunctional situation is in the case of Ken and Darlene. They brought their daughter, Sharon, in for therapy. She had a lifelong history of problems with anxiety and adjustment to new situations. She was finding their move to Grants Pass, Oregon to be a very difficult experience. Consequently, she was beginning to fall behind in school and was acting out her anger at home. Sharon repeatedly told and even yelled at her parents that she wanted to return to their home in the warmer southwestern part of our nation. Her parents were seriously considering putting in a request to the father's employer so they could return from whence they came. I informed them that such a move would be a major mistake and merely reinforce her irrational thinking and inappropriate behaviors.

Ken and Darlene agreed to attend a FAMILY seminar with their four children. When they implemented FAMILY in their home, Sharon became genuinely compliant and worked through her issues in therapy rather quickly. Once she realized that her manipulation tactics weren't going to work and that she was marooned in Grants Pass until high school graduation, she settled in and became more emotionally stable. I might add that medication helped her too.

The surprise for Ken, Darlene, and myself was the response of their son, Greg. His true colors came out because FAMILY provided more structure in the home and shed the light on his manipulation tactics with mom. He was getting away with subtle defiant behaviors because Sharon's antics provided a diversion for him. FAMILY shed the light on the cockroaches in Ken and Darlene's family kitchen and Greg's cockroach antennae were caught in the cookie jar. Darlene was confronted, by me, concerning her enabling and rescuing behaviors of her children. She decided to take a stand with Ken to confront Greg.

As a result of Ken and Darlene's united parental stand, Greg became superficially compliant for a few months. His parents were pleased and their family appeared to becoming more stable; however, they were merely in the eye of Hurricane Greg. A short time later, the torrential winds and rains of Hurricane Greg pounded down relentlessly on Ken and Darlene's shoreline. Greg was acting out with a vengeance. He made it clear that he was unwilling to submit himself to his parents' authority. School took a turn for the worse and he was getting into fights without remorse. He enjoyed it.

The straw that broke the camel's back for Ken and Darlene was when Greg had the audacity to file false complaints of physical abuse to school authorities. It was a desperate act on Greg's part to try and keep the upper hand with his parents. Unfortunately, this happens sometimes in families and the Child Protective Services agency treats the parents as if they are guilty until proven innocent. These state agencies are a necessary evil. They do help kids who are actually abused. Greg stated he hated his parents and siblings and did not care about what negative consequences his false allegation had on his parents' reputations or their careers. The matter was eventually cleared up and the truth prevailed. Greg also won an all expense paid trip to long-term residential treatment because of the "pop fly" he earned due to his false reporting. He was out of control in a major way. Ken, Darlene, and Sharon continued therapy and attended self-exploration seminars. Their new-found awareness of their own personal issues assisted them in becoming better human-beings as well as better parents. Greg successfully completed his treatment in Jamaica and the entire family is doing much better. No more cockroaches in the family kitchen.

FAMILY really works, just not always in the way that some parents would like it to; however, pest control is necessary to prevent the rats behind the walls from breeding. We don't need another generation of troubled adolescents. Finally, it's better to know what's going on at night in a bright kitchen than it is to step on the little buggers in the dark with your bare feet. Denial is yucky! Parenting is a challenge, but, if you're proactive, everyone wins in the end. You win, your children win, your school wins, your church or synagogue wins, your community wins, and our society wins. There's no place like home (click, click, click) to begin making the positive and healthy changes made possible by implementing FAMILY in your home. Goodbye rats and cockroaches! Hello FAMILY! It's time to turn your family right side up with the FAMILY of all parenting discipline systems, because "every home needs a FAMILY."

11 *Community Parenting*

YOU ARE TO BE commended for your obvious love and concern for your family and it's present and future well-being. You wouldn't be reading this book right now if this wasn't the case. We need many more proactive parents like you in our communities, involving themselves in the lives of their children. We need more parents who are constantly seeking to improve their family environment, staying on top of their children's behaviors, their whereabouts, and who their friends are. This is truly positive parenting. However, your responsibility does not end with your own family. You belong to a much larger family called a community. In spite of our society's technological progress and our subsequent tendency to become isolated and self-sufficient, we are responsible for our neighbor's children, too. We truly are our brother's keeper.

Don't panic! I'm not talking about Hillary Clinton's book, *It Takes a Village to Raise a Child* (i.e., "It Takes Big Brother [The Government] To Raise Your Child"). I'm not a supporter of government intervention in the lives of families. Granted, Child Protective Service agencies exist for a reason. Some children really do get abused and neglected by irresponsible parents. Those parents deserve to have their children taken away. Abused and neglected children really do need our help and an advocate. Okay, Child Protective Service agencies sometimes make mistakes and inappropriately intervene. Often this is due to false allegations made by a lying child who is battling for control with his or her parents. Unfortunately, the agency sometimes treats parents as if they are guilty until proven innocent. This is very troubling for all involved parties. However, Child Protective Service agencies are a necessary evil. If they didn't exist, who would take care of our community's abused and neglected children? Who would intervene on their behalf?

Nevertheless, the kind of community parenting I'm talking about is the kind that used to be common place in most of our country's communities several decades ago. Now it can only be found in smaller suburbs and rural communities, such as where we live in Grants Pass, Oregon. This is very sad. Community parenting went belly up in many larger communities due to increased population, technological and economic isolation, and because of the lack of involvement of parents who refuse to discipline their children (i.e., "Boys will be boys! Ha! Ha! He'll grow out of it. Besides, it's none of your business!"). Many parents gave up on reporting inappropriate behaviors of some children to their uninvolved apathetic parents because the parents wouldn't do anything about it.

In spite of this sad scenario, you can still do your small part in reviving this very valuable tradition of community interdependence. Children and adolescents need to know that if they misbehave in public, their parents will find out later because another concerned community parent will make sure they do. Our nation's courts and state legislatures are finally starting to crack down on these uninvolved apathetic parents—the ones who have no interest in knowing whether or not their children are drinking, taking drugs, stealing, building pipe bombs in the garage, or purchasing guns and hiding them in their bedrooms so they can shoot up the school later on. If you see a child or adolescent misbehaving, do something about it. Communicate with the child's parents and include an expectation that they do something about it. If the parents respond in an uninvolved apathetic manner, inform them that you will contact the police, make a report to the Child Protective Services agency, or confront them in civil court. Your proactive involvement in community parenting will inspire others, whether or not they want to be inspired, into holding up their end of the stick. We all need to be involved in our children's lives.

My first involvement in community parenting was when I was approximately four years old. I was spending a couple of days at my grandparents' home in Portland, Oregon. Fortunately, my parents left my tricycle for me to ride. I clearly remember my grandma telling me where I could ride my tricycle and where I couldn't ride it (i.e., down the steep hill). When grandma went inside her house, I rode my tricycle down the sidewalk to the top of the steep hill, double checked to make sure she wasn't looking, and went for the ride of my life. After going about one-hundred feet down the steep hill, I realized I had no brakes. The stop sign and busy intersection were quickly approaching. I turned into someone's driveway and smacked right into a concrete wall. I woke up a few minutes later with blood all over me. An adult male was carrying me and my tricycle back up the hill, trying to find out who was responsible for me. My grandma came running out of her house in a panic. Boy! Did he let my grandma have it! She never let me out of her sight after that. If that's not community parenting, I don't know what is.

Another experience in community parenting involved my looking out the front window of my house and seeing a ten year old boy start to beat up an eight year old boy. I opened up my front door and told him to stop. He ignored me and continued to hit the younger and smaller boy. I went out to the street and told him to stop. He said it was none of my business. As I was restraining him from beating up the younger child, I told him that it was my neighborhood and my driveway, therefore it was my business. I asked him where he lived and he wouldn't tell me. I told him if he didn't tell me, I was going to call the police. He told me where he lived. I walked this kid down the street back to his home. I rang the door bell and his mother opened it up. She was half drunk and looked surprised by my asking her to stay on top of her child's behaviors. She started to tell me that it was none of my business, but stopped when I told her I would call the police if she didn't change her tune. She complied and took her boy inside the house. He never fought in my neighborhood again. The younger boy played in peace and security because he knew a community parent cared enough to watch out for him.

Just prior to moving to Oregon, I had an experience involving community parenting while I was driving approximately 360 miles from Fairbanks to Anchorage along the Parks Highway. This is one of the most beautiful drives in Alaska and goes through the middle of the pristine wilderness, including incredible breathtaking views of Mt. McKinley and Denali National Park. It was early spring and still very cold. The sun was starting to go down. Well, smack dab in the middle of the 360 mile stretch of highway, I came across a broken down vehicle with five adolescents. They were heading toward Fairbanks. They informed me that they ran out of oil and that their engine seized up. They asked me if I had any oil and I told them that I didn't. The next stop was about 20 miles down the road. I drove south and was given oil by a very nice maintenance man at the Denali Princess Lodge. I was willing to pay for the oil but he refused to take the money after hearing why I needed it. He wasn't willing to charge a Good Samaritan who was trying to help out some desperate teens. I found out that there was a tow truck about 15 miles south of the lodge.

I drove 20 miles back north to deliver the oil to the stranded teens. It was nearly dark. They informed me that they obtained motor oil from a passing motorist and learned that their engine was no longer operating. One of the teens hopped in the passing motorist's car and headed north to a gas station 75 miles away. He did not know that there was a towing company 35 miles to the south. When you are stuck out in the middle of the wilderness in Alaska, every mile counts because towing a disabled vehicle is very expensive. Three teens climbed into my truck and one of them refused to get in. He thought he should stay with the car. I reminded him that it was almost dark and very cold. I told him that he had no heat because his car was disabled and that Honolulu, Hawaii was going to freeze over before I left him behind. I sternly told him to get in my truck so we could catch his friend before they traveled too far north. He complied and climbed into my truck.

While driving north to catch the passing motorist and their friend, the four teens in my truck caught me up to speed on how they ended up in their situation. Apparently, they were out and about having fun in Fairbanks and ended up violating their curfew. Instead of going home late and paying the piper, they impulsively decided to drive 360 miles south to Anchorage. They made it to Anchorage and spent the night in a hotel room. Keep in mind, they never called their parents. Not one of them. I'll tell you what, I'd be freaking out if one of them was my child. On their way back from Anchorage to Fairbanks, their car engine seized because they ran out of motor oil. Does this sound like a bunch of impulsively out of control adolescents or what?

After driving about 30 miles north, we caught up with the passing motorist and extracted the fifth adolescent from the car. I informed him that there was a towing company 35 miles south of their stranded car and that he would save a great deal of money by having them tow his car. He got in my truck and we drove 30 miles south back to their car. We stopped so they could get all of their personal possessions out. Then we drove 20 miles south to the Denali Princess Lodge where I could make a phone call to one of the teen's parents. I could only imagine how that parent felt when a stranger called, introducing himself as Dr. Johnson, and telling him about his teen's dilemma. I assured him that I would take care of his child and the other four teens. They weren't going to be left alone in the dark of night and the freezing Alaska outdoor temperatures.

We drove 15 more miles to the south. During our drive south, I informed the teens that they had better eat crow and humble pie when their parents arrive the next morning. One of the teens said, "Why should we. We didn't do anything wrong!" Two other teens spoke up and said, "Oh, yes we did. We broke curfew, left Fairbanks and drove to Anchorage without our parents' permission, and got ourselves stuck in the middle of nowhere. We're lucky "Dr. J." stopped to help us out or we'd be freezing to death! We did plenty wrong!" We found the towing company. Fortunately, the Texaco gas station in Trapper's Creek had a restaurant so the kids could go inside to eat a late dinner and stay warm.

The kids didn't have any money so I gave the cashier my credit card and told her to write down the appropriate information. I informed her that the adolescents' parents would be picking them up tomorrow morning and that they would pay for the dinner and breakfast when they arrived. If they didn't pay her, she could put the kid's meals on my credit card. It was about 11:00 P.M. and it was too late and too far for the parents to drive from Fairbanks. So the cashier fed the kids and helped me to find a local bed and breakfast in Trapper's Creek to put them up for the night.

I spoke to the tow truck driver and informed him of the stranded car's location approximately 20 miles to the north. I gave him my credit card information and informed him that the teens' parents would pay for the tow tomorrow morning. If they didn't pay for the towing, I told him to put it on my credit card. One of the boys hopped into the tow truck and drove north to retrieve his disabled vehicle.

When we arrived at the bed and breakfast, we were greeted by a very friendly older lady. I explained the situation to her and asked that she put the boys and girls in two separate rooms. She understood and told me that her room is located between their rooms. She assured me that there would be no inappropriate behaviors going on while she was on duty. I gave her my credit card information and informed her that the parents would pay for the rooms tomorrow morning when they arrived. I told her that if she was not paid, to charge the two rooms to my credit card. Fortunately, she was very willing to be flexible and help out the teens.

When I was saying my goodbyes to the teens at the bed and breakfast, they thanked me a thousand times. One of the girls stated, "You're Jesus Christ in the flesh, so loving and kind." Before I ducked out the door, I told her, "There's only one Jesus and I'm not him. However, I am a Christian and I believe in doing unto others as you would have others do unto you. If any of you were my kids, I would want someone to help you out in a time of need." They nodded their heads in agreement. Finally, I stated, "Please promise that you will do one favor for me." They responded, "What? We'll do anything!" I responded, "Please give your parents a big hug and apologize to them for what you did. Treat them with respect and don't mouth off to them in spite of the consequences you will receive and deserve." They gave me their word that they would remain humble in spirit. I arrived to my destination in Anchorage a few hours later than planned. However, I slept well knowing that the teens were safe and that I was practicing what I preached.

Three cheers to all of the individuals who participated in the above examples. If this isn't community parenting, I don't know what is. These five teens were impulsively getting themselves into deeper and deeper trouble as time passed. If it wasn't for the assistance of a flexible maintenance man, a passing motorist, a cashier, a tow truck driver, a bed and breakfast owner, and a traveling psychologist, these kids could have died from hypothermia before they knew what was happening.

Finally, one last example of community parenting that I experienced was when I took my son, Levi, to a local high school football game. As we approached the main entrance to the football stadium, we both saw a family friend standing outside the gate. Brian was smoking a cigarette with his other high school buddies. When Brian saw Levi and me, his face turned white and he had a "I'm busted" look on his face. I was shocked and walked right by Brian without saying a word. Brian knew I was upset.

The next morning, I made one of the most difficult phone calls I ever had to make in my life. I was uncertain whether or not Brian's parents knew that he was smoking cigarettes. They assured me that they were aware of his smoking problem but had no success in trying to get him to stop. Apparently, he just started smoking a few months prior to our seeing him outside the gate. They asked me if I would take their son, Brian, out to lunch and talk with him about my concerns. I agreed to do so and set up a lunch date that same day with Brian.

I met Brian at a local restaurant of his choice. We sat down and caught up on what was going on in our lives. While talking, we ordered lunch. I told Brian to order anything that he wanted to eat because lunch was on me. In addition to lunch, I also ordered a very large glass of beer. Brian's face had a major look of surprise on it when I ordered the beer. He knew that I didn't drink alcohol. We talked and ate our lunch for a good hour while the large glass of beer sat in the middle of the table. Occasionally, Brian would look at the glass of beer and then at me. I could tell that he was wondering if I was ever going to take a drink.

Finally, after much time had passed, I asked Brian, "Did you notice that I ordered a large glass of beer?" Brian replied, "Yes! You sure shocked me!" I asked Brian another question, "Did you notice that I never took a drink from the glass?" Brian said, "Yes, but I think it's okay for Christians to drink alcohol." I told him that I thought it was okay for Christians to drink alcohol too as long as it is in moderation. I also told Brian that I don't drink because alcoholism runs in my family and I don't want to take a chance at becoming an alcoholic. I asked Brian, "So, you were shocked when I ordered the beer, huh?" "Yes," replied Brian.

I informed Brian that Levi and I were equally shocked when we saw him smoking a cigarette outside the football stadium. In tears, I shared my concerns to Brian about the poor example he was setting for my son as well as the poor example he was setting for his younger siblings. I reminded Brian that Levi adores him and that it really threw him for a tail spin when he saw Brian smoking. I also expressed my concerns to Brian about what smoking will ultimately do to his health. I informed Brian that I was left with the unfortunate decision of not being able to take him with Levi and me from Fairbanks down to Anchorage to watch the Great Alaska Shootout during the Thanksgiving holiday (i.e., the best preseason collegiate basketball tournament in the nation). The three of us have made this trip a few times together during the Thanksgiving holidays. Both my tears and the harsh reality of missing out on a collegiate basketball junkie fix really shook Brian up.

Brian reached a point of tears and committed himself to abstinence from nicotine. He told me that he never thought about how his smoking might have a negative impact on Levi and his younger siblings. Brian had an epiphany. He realized just how self-centered he was being with his new found negative habit. He has remained abstinent from nicotine ever since our lunch date. We had a blast at the Great Alaska Shootout! There's no better way to spend a Thanksgiving holiday than watching four straight days of nonstop collegiate basketball from the front row seats located right on the half-court line. However, now that we have moved to Oregon, we are going to settle for watching the Oregon Ducks and Portland Trail Blazers basketball games. Great hoops!

Please dads and moms, practice community parenting. We all need one another. You might have to help one of my kids someday. If one of my kids are messing up, I want you to tell me. Let's work together to love and protect our children. Community parenting works!

Part 3
FAMILY Questions?

12 *Questions & Answers*

UNDOUBTEDLY, YOU HAVE nit-picky questions concerning the implementation of the FAMILY system. Well, there's good news! I am going to try my best to anticipate every single question you can think of about FAMILY, and attempt to answer those questions here and now. I'm also going to admit I'm 100% human and I'm going to forget to include a few questions and answers in this chapter. However, thanks to the modern miracles of technology, you will have the ability to contact my website and ask questions about FAMILY that I forgot to include in this chapter (www.family-rules.com). You may also send an e-mail message to me (drj@family-rules.com). I will post the answers to your questions on my website for you and others to see. Your name will not be included in order to protect your confidentiality. However, your city and State will be included so you know who it is. You will also have the opportunity to view questions asked by other parents that you didn't think about asking. I'll include all of those questions in the next edition of this book. On with the questions and answers.

A QUESTION CONCERNING A *FAMILY* GUARANTEE:

1. IS THE *FAMILY* SYSTEM GUARANTEED TO WORK WITH NO MORE PROBLEMS IN A SITUATION WHERE NO SYSTEM OF DISCIPLINE WAS IN PLACE - JUST CHAOS? No more problems? Wherever you find human parents and children, I guarantee you will find problems. However, if you correctly and consistently implement FAMILY in your home (i.e., "the two 'C' words"), you will find that the chaos will diminish to a relatively sane level of tolerance. Don't forget the stalled car analogy mentioned earlier in the book.

QUESTIONS ABOUT CORPORAL PUNISHMENT:

1. SHOULD A PARENT PUT SPANKING ON THE LIST OF RULES, RESERVING THE RIGHT TO IMPLEMENT THIS? No! I made it pretty clear, earlier in the book, that FAMILY is for children from Kindergarten through the 12th grade. These children are too old to spank! Time outs and limited spanking (i.e., one to three light swats on the rear without using an object - don't leave marks or bruises) are appropriate for children from age two through preschool. Once they reach kindergarten, don't spank them anymore! FAMILY will help to correct their behaviors if you implement the system correctly and consistently (i.e., "the two 'C' words"). Check out your state laws and/or consult with your attorney about spanking.

QUESTIONS ABOUT GOOD HABIT CARDS:

1. MY WIFE AND I WERE UNDER THE IMPRESSION THAT THE KIDS ONLY RECEIVED ONE CARD OR CARDS, DEPENDING ON WHAT WE SET, IF THEY DO NOT COMPLETE THEIR CHORES. Most families give one card per incomplete chore. Some families choose to give two good habit cards per incomplete chore.

2. ARE WE TO GIVE A CARD OR CARDS PER CHORE LEFT INCOMPLETE? Yes!!! Most families give only one card per incomplete chore (please read above question).

3. WHAT IF SOMEONE PULLS A CARD, THEN SOMEONE ELSE BREAKS A RULE AND PULLS THE SAME CARD? CAN WE PUT IT BACK? When a good habit card has been pulled and completed, place it in the discard pile. No one else should be able to pull this card again until the rest of the cards have been completed and end up in the discard pile. When all the cards have been completed and are placed in the discard pile, reshuffle them and start all over again.

4. WHAT IF SOMEONE HAS ALL 50 CARDS, AND THEN SOMEBODY ELSE BREAKS THE RULE? Give the second offender their good habit cards from the stack of 50 cards. Once they have been completed, put them back into the stack of 50 cards. The individual who has 50 cards to do will still have to do all 50 cards. So what if some of the cards were just done! The toilet, stove, or kitchen floor can't be cleaned too many times.

5. IF THE PARENT FEELS THAT ON ONE OCCASION TOO MANY GOOD HABIT CARDS WERE GIVEN, IS IT APPROPRIATE NEXT TIME TO DECREASE THE NUMBER OF GOOD HABIT CARDS GIVEN? One of the great things about the FAMILY system is it tends to limit the influence of emotions on parent's decision about discipline. Please take note that nowhere in the "Mechanics of FAMILY" section did you read where a parent's "feelings" play a role in determining how many cards a child receives or doesn't receive. Once again, the number of good habit cards are predetermined and placed within the parenthesis next to the numbered rules. When a child or adult breaks the rule, he or she receives the number of good habit cards adjacent to the rule. No more and no less. Please implement FAMILY the way you were taught and don't deviate from the program because of the way you feel. If you allow your feelings to dictate your decisions, then you will undermine your own authority. Also, if you give one child a break, the other children will want breaks too. If you don't give them the same break, then you will be accused of favoring one child over another. Just stick with the program and set your feelings aside. Remember, you are conducting business. Parenting business.

6. IS IT OKAY TO START LOW, LIKE 1 OR 2 GOOD HABIT CARDS, AND GRADUALLY INCREASE THE NUMBER OF CARDS WITH EACH OFFENSE? Yes and no. As I stated in a previous answer, please start off low and work your way up from there. However, you should not increase the number of cards with each offense. You should give your children time to see if their behaviors settle down. If a certain rule continues to be broken after some time has lapsed, then consult with your spouse and increase the number of cards. Remember, you both have to be in agreement before you raise the number of good habit cards.

7. BECAUSE SOME CHORES NEED TO BE DONE MORE OFTEN THAN OTHERS, CAN THE PARENT SUBSTITUTE CHORES WHEN GOOD HABIT CARDS ARE DRAWN? Yes, but only when a "Wild Card" is drawn. Otherwise, stick to the good habit cards drawn. Please remember to implement the FAMILY system correctly and consistently. Don't deviate from the program for the sake of convenience. Remember, if you choose to have the rule, "Do what you're asked to do immediately without complaining," on your list, then you can simply ask them to do the chore. Also, don't forget to make up a list of daily and weekly chores.

8. IS IT OKAY TO HAVE MORE THAN 50 GOOD HABIT CARDS IN A STACK? Yes. You can have 500 good habit cards in a stack. However, no child or adult can ever have more than 50 cards total. I learned about 800 families ago that more than 50 cards is seen by children as too deep of a hole to dig themselves out.

9. IF WE AS PARENTS HAVE A HECTIC SCHEDULE, CAN WE SET A TIME LIMIT WHEN WE NEED THE CARDS DONE? No. As I explained earlier in the book, the children are now in charge of whether or not they are grounded and for how long they are grounded. When they choose to break a rule or not get their chore done, they are choosing to ground themselves. When they are grounded, they have two choices: (1) Get their good habit cards done right away, or (2) Stay in their room until they choose to leave their room and complete their good habit cards. Please don't allow your hectic lifestyle to undermine your parenting priorities. Cut back on your schedule if it is interfering with your most important responsibility - your kids.

10. ARE CHILDREN ALLOWED TO DO THEIR GOOD HABIT CARDS WHEN IT IS BEDTIME? No. If they still have good habit cards at bedtime, then the cards carry over to the next day. Don't allow your children to manipulate their bedtimes. This will motivate them to get their cards done before bedtime.

11. WHAT IS THE DIFFERENCE BETWEEN BREAKING THE RULES AND PULLING GOOD HABIT CARDS AND NOT COMPLETING CHORES AND PULLING GOOD HABIT CARDS? When a child breaks a rule, they are to receive the predetermined number of good habit cards found in the parenthesis adjacent to the numbered rule. When a child does not complete a chore, they normally receive one good habit card per incomplete chore. A few families decide to give two good habit cards per incomplete chore.

12. SHOULD WE HAVE A TOTAL OF 55 CARDS IN THE DECK, INCLUDING WILD AND GRACE CARDS? Yes. There are a total of 50 cards in a deck that can be completed. This number includes the "Wild Cards." The "Grace Cards" are an additional five cards to the deck and therefore the total number of cards in the deck is 55. But, you can't do a "Grace Card" because it simply lets the child or adult off the hook for that particular card.

13. IF YOU HAVE LIMITED WAYS TO GET GOOD HABIT CARDS, CAN YOU CHANGE THE RULES TO ALLOW DAILY/WEEKLY CHORES TO ACQUIRE GOOD HABIT CARDS? As previously explained in the book and in this question and answer chapter, most families give one good habit card per incomplete chore. A few families choose to give two good habit cards per incomplete chore.

14. IF YOU HAVE MULTIPLE CARDS, BUT YOU GET A GRACE CARD, SHOULD YOUR CARDS BE CANCELLED? No. If you receive five good habit cards and one of those cards is a "Grace Card," then you only get off the hook for that one card. You still have to do the other four cards.

15. WHAT IF THE CHILD WRITES OR SCRIBBLES ON A GOOD HABIT CARD? Messing with the FAMILY system in any way results in the child receiving all 50 cards. They are not to mess with the lists, cards, or chips! No! No!

QUESTIONS ABOUT RAK CHIPS AND REWARD TOKENS:

1. CAN WE PUT A LIMIT ON RAK CHIPS? Yes. However, lean in the direction of graciously rewarding your children for their kindness. All too often, parents naturally focus on their children's negative behaviors while taking their children's positive behaviors for granted. Let them know you appreciate their Random Acts of Kindness.

2. HOW MANY REWARDS SHOULD BE ON THE LIST, AND CAN WE HAVE A SEPARATE REWARDS LIST FOR EACH CHILD? There is no minimum or maximum number of rewards required on the list. It's up to you. You need to determine how much time and financial resources you have available to provide the rewards. Yes. You may have separate reward lists for your children.

3. READING THROUGH THE BOOK, I NOTICED A FEW THINGS THAT WERE NOT MENTIONED. MY QUESTION FOR YOU IS WE HAVE NOT BEEN GIVING THE KIDS RAK CHIPS FOR DAILY CHORES. YOU NEVER MENTIONED IT (OR WE DON'T REMEMBER) SO I WANT TO KNOW IF WE SHOULD INITIATE THIS PRACTICE? No. Doing their daily and weekly chores and not breaking the rules is rewarded with a daily FAMILY token at night time just before they go to bed. Give your children RAK chips for Random Acts of Kindness - not daily and weekly chore requirements (i.e., my daughter made the bed for her brother because he flew out of the house this morning. She did it out of the kindness of her heart without being asked. She gets a RAK chip. He gets cards when he gets home for not completing his chore).

4. IF WE DO INITIATE THIS PRACTICE, DO WE GIVE THEM ANY REMINDERS (REFER TO QUESTION #1)? CAN WE SUBSTITUTE A REMINDER FOR A RAK CHIP OR VICE VERSA? No. Please remember to correctly and consistently implement the FAMILY system as explained. Deviations from the organization and structure of FAMILY cause the program to collapse.

5. SHOULD WE REWARD A CHILD WITH GOOD GRADES WITH A SECOND CHILD WHO HAS LEARNING DISABILITIES? Once again, FAMILY is flexible - not rigid. You can write rules that apply to both of your children's unique learning abilities as you see fit. Just make sure that you are both in agreement before you write down the rule.

QUESTIONS ABOUT STRIKES:

1. IF THE CHILD IS DEFIANT AND NOT WILLING TO COMPLY WITH THE RULE, AT WHAT POINT IN TIME DOES THAT BECOME A STRIKE? When a child continues to defy a parents authority over an extended period of time, they are pushing their luck and may receive a strike. Please go back to "Y" and read the difference between a strike and a bad hair day. Also, check out the information on pop-flies. In a nutshell, if a child makes it clear via their body language, words, and actions that Honolulu, Hawaii will freeze over first before they will obey their mom and dad, then they will receive a strike. Consult with an objective third party before giving your child a "strike."

QUESTIONS ABOUT YOUNGER CHILDREN:

1. IS IT OKAY TO NEGOTIATE HAVING THE PARENT HELP THE CHILD WHEN THE JOB IS TOO DIFFICULT FOR A YOUNGER CHILD TO DO? Yes. However, to avoid this problem, consider creating two separate decks of 50 good habit cards. One deck of 50 good habit cards can be used by the older children and adults. The other deck of 50 good habit cards can be used by the younger children. This second deck of good habit cards can consist of easier activities to do for the younger children. Finally, it's okay to jump in the tub the first couple of times, with your kids, and teach them how to clean it. After the initial instruction, they will be on their own.

2. WITH SMALL CHILDREN, IS IT WISE TO START THE FIRST FEW DAYS WITH DAILY TOKENS AND REWARDS BEFORE USING GOOD HABIT CARDS? Yes! Let them taste the sweet before they taste the sour. The daily tokens, rewards, and RAK chips help the children to buy into the FAMILY system. You can do this for up to one week. Then the good habit cards need to begin.

3. WHEN CHOOSING THE NUMBER OF GOOD HABIT CARDS, SHOULD AGE OF THE CHILDREN BE A FACTOR? No. The number of good habit cards should be predetermined by the parent(s) ahead of time and placed within the parenthesis, next to the numbered rules, on the family's list of household rules. Keep in mind that you want to start off low (i.e., 1 to 3 cards) and work your way up from there. However, start with a large number of cards for the most important rules (i.e., Obey all local, state, federal, and military laws, etc.). Don't forget, you can have two separate decks of good habit cards: one deck of 50 good habit cards for the older children and the adults and a different deck of 50 good habit cards for the younger children.

4. WHAT DO YOU DO WITH A YOUNG CHILD WHO DELIBERATELY BREAKS THE RULES JUST TO GET ANOTHER CARD? Some young children have fun doing the good habit cards and like the attention they receive in the process. Don't worry, the novelty of FAMILY will wear off. They will stop. A positive alternative is to inform them that they can do chores around the home without breaking the rules. Offer them RAK chips for doing chores. Remind them that they lose their daily chip if they break the rules or do not complete their chores. Finally, as previously mentioned, if a child continues to break a certain rule on a continuous basis, then consult with your spouse and increase the number of good habit cards.

5. SHOULD THE PARENT GIVE A YOUNG CHILD ALL 50 CARDS TO DO WITHIN A WEEK IF HE CONTINUES TO BREAK THE SAME RULES REPETITIVELY? Don't allow yourself to be manipulated by guilt. If your child earns all 50 cards, then give them 50 cards. Let them experience the natural consequences of their choices. Don't bail them out. Otherwise, you are enabling them to become a defiant monster. Remind them about strikes and pop-flies.

6. CAN YOU ADJUST THE CARDS FOR THE YOUNGER KIDS AND ONE FOR THE OLDER KIDS? Yes. You can have a deck of cards for the older kids and adults, as well as a deck of cards for the younger kids. FAMILY is flexible.

7. IS CRYING OVER A PULLED CARD CONSIDERED IMPOLITE? No! Defiance and rudeness are impolite! Let the tears flow without consequences; however, absolutely do not allow your child to guilt trip you with their tears. Remember "the two 'C' words" - correct and consistent implementation.

8. WHEN I WAS A KID, THERE WERE SOME INSTANCES WHEN IT SEEMED LIKE I JUST COULDN'T HELP CRYING. Me too!! I was a big cry baby sometimes. I still am at times. Don't repress your child's tears.

9. WHEN CHILDREN ARE OVERLY TIRED, SHOULD THE PARENT SHOW GRACE WHEN THEY ACT OUT? I don't know about you, but I can be a grouch sometimes when I'm tired. However, being tired is no excuse for inappropriate behaviors. It's okay to use your parental wisdom and bestow grace upon your children once in a while. Please be careful! Make sure you don't bestow too much continual grace upon your children. You may end up teaching them that it's okay to misbehave if they are tired. They need to get a grip on their emotions, even when they are tired.

10. IS IT OKAY TO REMIND THE KIDS ABOUT THEIR CHORES OR SHOULD WE ZIP A LIP SO THEY PRACTICE RESPONSIBIL- ITY? A little bit of grace at first wouldn't hurt, but only for the first week of implementation at the most. Then zip the lip so they learn responsibility.

QUESTIONS ABOUT OLDER CHILDREN/ADOLESCENTS:

1. IF YOU HAVE AN 18-YEAR-OLD, MATURE, COMPLIANT, AND OBEDIENT TEENAGER WHO IS DOING WELL BEFORE *FAM- ILY* WAS IMPLEMENTED, SHOULD YOU MAKE HIM ADHERE TO THE FAMILY SYSTEM, ESPECIALLY WITH TWO YOUNGER CHILDREN IN THE HOME? Your 18-year-old is an adult just like you. You are much older and hopefully were mature and compli- ant before FAMILY was implemented in your home. Nevertheless, you are adhering to the FAMILY system and so should your 18- year-old. When your children turn 18, they change to the status of a tenant. If the tenant doesn't obey the landlord's rules, the tenant is evicted. After the 18-year-old graduates from high school, he doesn't receive daily tokens or RAK chips, but he does receive the good habit cards. Finally, if your 18-year-old is truly mature, com- pliant, and obedient, he or she won't have any problems with adhering to the FAMILY system just like you have to do. Other- wise, if there is a problem with adhering to the FAMILY system, then I guess the teenager wasn't so mature, compliant, and obedi- ent after all.

2. IS THERE DANGER IN PARENTS USING THEIR AUTHORITY TO CHALLENGE THE WISHES OF A BRIGHT, RESPECTFUL, AND OLDER ADOLESCENT, FORCING HIM OR HER TO OBEY THEM? You are joking, right? Please reverse the question. Is there danger in allowing a bright, respectful, and older adolescent to disobey his or her parents? If this child is truly respectful, then this shouldn't really be an issue. They will naturally obey.

3. AT WHAT AGE SHOULD YOU ALLOW CHILDREN TO PUR- SUE THEIR OWN INTERESTS? You should be helping your children pursue their own interests from the time they are knee high to a grasshopper. Allow them to explore new areas of interest throughout their years at home as long as it is legal, ethical, and moral. However, if their own interests are alcohol, drugs, sex, and gangs, you better put your foot down.

4. SHOULD YOU HAVE DIFFERENT RULES REGARDING TELE-PHONE USE FOR DIFFERENT CHILDREN, DEPENDING ON THE CHILD BEING COMPLIANT, HAVING GOOD GRADES, ETC.? As explained earlier in the book, FAMILY is a skeletal framework of organization and structure. You get to slap the meat and skin on it to reflect your unique morals and values. No two families are the same. FAMILY is flexible - not rigid. If you want to craft a family rule with your spouse that covers the above issue, go for it! You can word a rule anyway you want to as long as both parents are in agreement.

5. SHOULD YOU STOP THE *FAMILY* SYSTEM AT THE AGE OF 18 EVEN THOUGH THE CHILD IS STILL IN HIGH SCHOOL AND LIVING AT HOME? Earlier in the book, I talked about taking the medication until it is all gone. Please remember, the medication is not all gone until the last child turns 18, graduates from high school, and moves out of your home. At age 18, high school graduate or not, he or she becomes a tenant as well. If the child continually disobeys you, evict him or her from the premises! You can't permit the 18-year-old to set a bad example for the young ones.

6. WE HAD AN INCIDENT TODAY WHERE ONE OF THE KIDS LEFT TRASH IN THE OFFICE. WHEN I QUESTIONED EACH OF MY FAMILY MEMBERS, EACH ONE REPLIED THAT HE OR SHE DID NOT LEAVE THE TRASH. CONSIDERING THE LACK OF OFFICE USE, THAT WRAPPER COULD HAVE BEEN SIT-TING THERE FOR DAYS AND KNOWING MY FAMILY, SOME-BODY PROBABLY REALLY CAN'T REMEMBER. WHAT SHOULD I DO? GIVE EVERYBODY A CARD OR LET IT GO? Let it go. Exercise grace and wisdom in this matter. If it were ketchup all over the kitchen floor and counters, you might want to turn up the heat — but not for one wrapper left a couple of days ago. Pick and choose your battles wisely.

7. WHEN A CHILD IS NOT ACTING CORRECTLY, HAS BROKEN A RULE, AND WANTS TO TALK AND EXPLAIN OR ASK QUESTIONS, DO YOU ALLOW THE CHILD TO TALK OR MAKE HIM OR HER WAIT UNTIL THE WEEKLY FAMILY MEETING? This is another opportunity for your use of parental wisdom, grace, and discretion. If your child is a defiant little brat who is simply engaged in disrespectful back talk, then make the child wait until after completing the good habit cards. If he or she doesn't do the good habit cards politely, keep on doubling them until the child is polite, but don't forget to give them a 10-minute cooling period in between the doubling of the cards. On the other hand, if your child is fairly mature and responsible and wouldn't normally want to talk or explain his or her behavior, then you best give him or her your ear for a few minutes — not hours. You might possibly have made a mistake in judgment. Be fair, but don't be an enabler of parental disrespect.

QUESTIONS ABOUT PARENTAL CONSEQUENCES:

1. CAN A PARENT BE GROUNDED? Yes. If a parent breaks a family rule, then he or she is grounded until the good habit cards are completed. The parent needs to be working on the cards or sitting in the bedroom until ready to complete the cards.

2. WHAT HAPPENS IF ONE PARENT REQUESTS A JOB TO BE DONE IMMEDIATELY THAT CAUSES EVERYONE ELSE TO BREAK ONE OR MORE RULES, SUCH AS BEING ON TIME? If a parent pulls rank and places a demand on the family that causes them to break a rule, such as being on time, then they are off the hook. Otherwise, we have a pretty unfair and inconsistent parent at the helm who needs a reality check.

3. WOULD IT BE A MINOR INFRACTION TO ROLL THROUGH A STOP SIGN IF YOU WERE GOING SLOW? The law is the law. A policeman would give you a ticket for this offense except in New Jersey. In New Jersey, motorists speed down the side street and through the stop sign just to get in front of you. They don't know what the word "stop" means in New Jersey. If your parents have a rule on the list about obeying all laws, then you will receive the number of good habit cards found in the parenthesis adjacent to the numbered rule. Parents receive cards too if they roll through stop signs.

4. IF A PARENT IS GROUNDED, DOES HE OR SHE GET TO TAKE A LONG- DISTANCE PHONE CALL FROM MOM? No. The grounded parent should complete any good habit cards first or sit in the bedroom until he or she decides to complete the cards. No phone calls until the cards are done.

5. DO PARENTS HAVE TO GO TO LONG-TERM RESIDENTIAL TREATMENT? No. Long-term residential treatment is only for children who disobey their parents over and over again. However, I have met many parents who wouldn't mind being sent to long-term residential treatment.

.

QUESTIONS ABOUT TWO HOMES DUE TO A DIVORCE:

1. WHAT SHOULD OR COULD WE DO TO MAKE THE TRANSITION SMOOTHER IF THE *FAMILY* SYSTEM IS ALREADY BEING DONE IN MY EX-SPOUSE'S HOME FOR THE CHILD? Great question! Unfortunately, divorces stink for everyone, especially the children. They end up being shuffled between two homes and receive mixed messages galore. This becomes really complicated when the ex-spouses are at war with one another. The children end up in the crossfire. Fortunately, I have worked with several ex-spouses who were willing to remain cordial with one another for the sake of their children. I have had plenty of blended families in my private practice setting and at my seminars who worked together to create a list of rules equally applied in both homes. As a result, the children are provided with much more consistency between the two homes and their transition becomes smoother. If you can attend counseling and avoid a divorce, please do it. If not, please work together with your ex-spouse to develop a list of FAMILY rules that will be implemented in both homes.

2. IN A TWO-HOUSEHOLD SITUATION, IF MAYBE 30 OF THE CARDS ARE THE SAME, CAN YOU TAKE ALONG THOSE 30 CARDS TO THE OTHER HOUSEHOLD? Yes. Consistency between the two homes is a must for the sake of the children. If you can maintain a cordial relationship with your ex-spouse for the sake of your children, please do so. This way your children can't divide and conquer.

3. IN A DIVORCED (TWO-FAMILY) SITUATION, COULD A CHILD DRAW TWO CARDS AT ONE HOME, AND WIND UP GOING TO THE OTHER HOME AND DRAW 50 CARDS THERE, TOO? If both parents are working together to maintain consistency between the two homes, then the answer to this question is yes. You simply take your 50 cards to the other parent's home and work on them there or stay in your bedroom. However, if both parents are using the FAMILY system but they aren't working together to maintain consistency between the two homes, then the answer to this question is no. Unfortunately, you will have 50 cards to do at both homes.

QUESTIONS ABOUT SINGLE PARENTS:

1. IS *FAMILY* JUST FOR MARRIED COUPLES OR CAN SINGLE PARENTS IMPLEMENT IT IN THEIR HOME TOO? Forgive me. I know I keep talking in terms of couples. Yes. Single parents can implement FAMILY in their home just as successfully as a married couple. Please assume that anything I write about married couples applies to you, too. However, since you don't have a spouse to consult with, you might want to consider consulting with an adult who's judgment you trust (i.e., a neighbor, family member, coworker, pastor, rabbi, milkman, etc.).

A QUESTION ABOUT SCHEDULING *FAMILY* SEMINARS:

1. HOW DO I SCHEDULE A *FAMILY* SEMINAR IN MY COMMUNITY? Contact me ("Dr. J.") via the following phone number: 1-541-956-8585. You may also contact me by my e-mail address (drj@family-rules.com). Finally, don't forget to check out the FAMILY Rules website (www.family-rules.com) to see if a FAMILY Rules seminar is already scheduled in your community.

A QUESTION ABOUT STARTING A *FAMILY* SUPPORT GROUP:

1. HOW DO I START A *FAMILY* SUPPORT GROUP MEETING IN MY COMMUNITY? Contact me at my private practice phone number, e-mail address, or website listed above. Check out the website because we might have an already established FAMILY support group in your community. If you want to start a support group, we will list it on the FAMILY Rules website.

QUESTIONS ABOUT "FAMILY Rules COUNSELORS":

1. WE WOULD LIKE OUR THERAPIST TO BECOME A "FAMILY-RULES COUNSELOR." HOW CAN THIS HAPPEN? Have your counselor contact me at the FAMILY Rules, Inc. office number (1-541-956-8585), e-mail address (drj@family-rules.com), or have the counselor check out my website (www.family-rules.com).

2. WE ARE SEEING A COUNSELOR AND WOULD LIKE TO IMPLEMENT *FAMILY RULES* IN OUR HOME. WHAT IF OUR COUNSELOR ADVISES US NOT TO DO SO? Your counselor knows your family situation better than I do. Please review chapters 4 through 7 with your counselor. If you have unresolved issues in your life, marriage, or family, you had better wait to implement FAMILY in your home. However, this is America and you do have freedom of choice. If your counselor leans in the direction of democratic parenting, you can choose to see a new counselor that offers a different approach. This is your consumer right.

Part 4
Appendices

A How to Become A FAMILY Rules Counselor

If you are a licensed clinician (i.e., LMFT, Clinical Social Worker, Psychologist, Psychiatrist, etc.) and/or an ordained clergyman, and you want to become a "FAMILY Rules Counselor," please contact Dr. Matthew A. Johnson via the following options:

Office Number: 1-(541)-956-8585
E-mail Address: drj@family-rules.com
Fax Number: 1-(541)-955-7165

What are the benefits of becoming a "FAMILY Rules Counselor?" Well, to begin with, you get to receive very practical training that will help you teach the organization and structure that most families need. Second, as a "FAMILY Rules Counselor," you get to have your name placed on the FAMILY Rules website referral page. Readers of the book, *FAMILY Rules*, will be able to access the website and find your name and office location. You will be allowed to have a link from the FAMILY Rules web site to your website provided your website is ethical and is done in good taste. Finally, you will be able to get families in and out of your office quicker (2-5 months) which will please the managed care companies. Prolonged therapy sessions will become a thing of the past. Yes, this will eat into your business profits initially; however, the increased number of referrals you will receive as a result usually makes up the difference.

Training consists of a six-hour seminar. Dr. Matthew A. Johnson can travel to your community and train multiple clinicians and/or clergy or you can contact him and travel with a group of clinicians and/or clergy to Grants Pass, Oregon. This may help you write off a part of your Oregon vacation. There's great fishing and hiking in Oregon! Lots to see and do. Talk with your accountant about the tax laws.

B-1

A Parent's FAMILY Testimonial

I TOLD DR. JOHNSON that I would be glad to write a testimonial about FAMILY, so here it is: When I found out I was pregnant with my first child, I swore that I would raise my children and react differently than my parents did with me. I can always remember when I was a child with my brother in the back seat of the car. It would start off with my brother breathing on me and then I would poke him and then he would start to whine. Sometime during the duration of this conflict my mother, who was driving, would keep one hand on the wheel of the car and with the other hand reach back and flail it wherever, hoping to hit someone in the process. I especially noticed the veins on her neck popping out. I told myself, I would NEVER be like that.

Thirty years later, I found myself doing the exact same thing. Despite reading *Dare to Discipline* and taking a number of parenting seminars, I found myself with bulging veins and having to repeat everything I said ten times because the kids seemed to be hearing impaired. I felt unappreciated and whatever happened would snowball emotionally until I blew up and got very angry with my children. I also found that my husband had a different set of rules with punishment. It seemed that he would become unglued over little things that the kids did that were due to childhood stupidity but the big things, like willful disobedience, did not merit severe consequences.

I honestly felt like I was a maid cleaning up after everyone's messes and no one seemed to respect the work I did in the house. Then there was the lack of respect of each child toward his siblings. I knew there had to be a way to teach children responsibility, both in the house and in terms of their behaviors. Then we went to a FAMILY seminar. Boy, have our lives changed!

First of all, I am not going to tell you that it is easy. It takes commitment and consistency—especially from the parents who have to work as a team. However, I feel that I can say I am a fair and objective parent. Any "punishment" my children have been given has been at their own hands. I have been able to sit back, point to the house rules, and put the responsibility of their woes on them. My house has never been cleaner and I feel that my children, both boys and girls, are learning lifetime skills that they will need when they live on their own (e.g., cooking, cleaning, washing, etc.). They are learning to interact as well as not to react to their siblings. Our house has been so much more peaceful, my husband and I are more united, and our children have grown because of the implementation of FAMILY in our home. The veins in my neck don't bulge and I feel I am a much better parent than I was nine months ago.

The final point that I would like to make is that my children know that there are consequences for their chosen behavior. They are assuming responsibility for their actions and not blaming anyone else. This, to me, is the basis of character. FAMILY has brought us closer together and is helping me to raise men and women, not boys and girls.

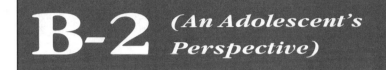

B-2 *(An Adolescent's Perspective)*

Before I went to long-term residential treatment at Paradise Cove in Western Samoa, I would explode with anger at almost anything. This I attributed to drugs, which I did every day during the last summer before I left home for Paradise Cove. I stole money from home. I smoked weed and drank a lot. My parents did not know about this. I was also smoking cigarettes for about six years. I didn't care about anything. Whenever something didn't go my way, I got mad and yelled and hit things or I ran away. My older brother and I got in a lot of fights. When he told on me for smoking, I ran downstairs and got a baseball bat and hit him three times. Mom had the police called, and we fought until the police showed up. I went to jail overnight, since formal charges were made against me. I got kicked out of school because of drugs. That was all my life revolved around.

When my parents first sent me to long-term residential treatment, I was so mad at them that I just wanted them to die or something. I couldn't see the things that I was doing when I yelled at them. It just made me hate them more. As I was being escorted out the front door of my parent's home to catch my plane, I yelled at them that I hated them and that they would never see me again.

While I was at Paradise Cove in Western Samoa, I learned a lot about the pain that I caused my parents and the pain that I didn't deal with myself. This also opened me up to see and change what I was doing to make my life better. It helped me to see that I didn't have to be a failure and a messed up person. I could live happy and deal with things that bother me in a different way.

Since I got home three months ago, things have been great and I am building more and more trust every day. I am really happy for once. I am building my relationships stronger every day and we all get along. I am having fun with my family.

Well, now I thank my parents for sending me there and loving me enough to do that. I know that it was as hard for them to send me there as it was for me to be there. All in all, I love them for doing it. Going to long-term residential treatment did save my life. I was in the fast lane and heading for a ditch a couple of times. I did almost die. I almost died from alcohol and driving high; also just smoking cigarettes (which I quit).

I think that if your child is out of control in your eyes then it would be good, for both the child and the parents, for the child to be treated. I know that there are also things that you can't or don't want to see your child doing. There is probably a lot you don't see and know about. You could save your child's life and improve your life. You can help your child.

B-3 *(An Adolescent's Perspective)*

Dear Dr. J.

I hate you! You screwed up my life and me.

Ever get a letter like that from someone you escorted to a program? I'll be honest, I wanted to write a letter like that, but I guess I never got to it. I'm glad that I didn't though. This program has helped me out a lot and I don't regret having to come here anymore.

Anyway, I met the latest <u>victim</u> you brought here. Guess what? He's in my family. I remember him from home, also. We didn't get along too well, but since I've changed we seem to get along fine now.

So how are things with you? I'm doing well here. Still level 3. I keep choosing out of the Accountability Seminar, but will have another chance soon, and this time I should do well. I was Assistant Family Leader for awhile which helped me out a lot, but no longer do I have the position, which is fine with me.

Well that's it I guess. I just wrote to say "hi." Adios! Have a happy Thanksgiving!

> Your Friend,
>
> (Name withheld to protect confidentiality.)

C

A Sample List of FAMILY Rules

The __(Family Name Here)__ **FAMILY Rules**

Good Habit Cards

(50)   1. Obey all local, state, federal, and military laws.

(1)   2. Do what you are asked to do immediately without complaining.

(1)   3. "No!" means "No!" Don't ask again.

(1)   4. Don't interrupt others. Wait your turn to talk.

(10)   5. Treat people and animals with respect (e.g., no verbal or physical abuse of others).

(3)   6. Obey all authority at home, school, church, synagogue, and in the community.

(2)   7. When you are angry, talk with an adult. Don't act out your anger inappropriately.

(1)   8. No inappropriate facial expressions or body gestures.

(5)   9. No stealing (i.e., borrowing without permission from the owner is stealing).

(10)   10. You must receive parental permission before you go anywhere at anytime.

(10)   11. You must stay where you receive permission to go. If plans change, call and ask parents.

(50)   12. Never run away from anywhere unless you have been abducted and/or are in danger.

(3)   13. No swearing or talking about inappropriate subject matter.

(10)   14. Parents' room is off limits. Knock and ask for parental permission before entering.

(2)   15. No eavesdropping on private parental conversations.

(20)   16. No lying, sneaking, or cheating (i.e., dishonest behaviors will not be tolerated).

(50)   17. No destruction of property regardless of who it belongs to.

(5)   18. No getting up at night to eat, watch TV, or to use the telephone or computer.

(3)   19. No eating certain foods when it has been explained to you that you are not to eat it.

(30)   20. No playing with matches or lighters (Use of such items with parental permission only).

(2)   21. Do not overuse your bathroom time or lock the door to keep others out. Be considerate.

(5)   22. Participate appropriately in family devotions and meetings (e.g., no joking, no mocking).

(10)   23. No use of telephone or computer without parental permission and parental supervision.

(2)   24. Do not keep others waiting when it is time to leave to go somewhere. Be on time.

(20)   25. No use of make up and/or jewelry without parental permission.

(1)   26. Always sleep with sheet on bed. Don't sleep in your regular street clothes.

(1)   27. No dishes, food, or trash left in the living room or your bedroom.

(1)   28. Eat with good manners.

(50)   29. No sexual activities with another person unless you are married to them.

(10)   30. Follow all school rules, obey all school personnel, and be on time to school and all classes.

(5)   31. No listening to inappropriate music or watching inappropriate videos or movies.

(5)   32. No faking sick or insisting on staying home from school.

(10)   33. Bring homework home from school. Don't forget!

(10)   34. Do all homework on time and turn it in on time.

(2)   35. Don't leave clothes, shoes, lunch utensils, or other personal belongings at school.

(10)   36. Obey all bus rules.

(5)   37. Behave appropriately at church/synagogue and follow parental directions. Sit with parents in church/synagogue.

(2)   38. Behave appropriately in the car. Don't play inside or on top of the car.

(1)   39. Complete all daily and weekly chores on time.

(3)   40. Attend all scheduled appointments on time and without complaining.

(10)   41. Take all medication as prescribed.

(➤)   42. You shall receive the following rewards and consequences for grades: A+ = $8; A = $7; A- = $6 B+ = $5; B = $4; B- = $3; C+ = $2; C = $1; C- = 0; D+ = 4 cards; D= 8 cards; D- = 12 cards; F= 20 cards.

(➤)   43. School year curfews are: 9:00 P.M. (Sun - Thurs nights) and 11:00 P.M. (Fri & Sat nights). Summer curfews are: 10:00 P.M. (Sun - Thurs nights) and 12 midnight (Fri & Sat nights). You will receive 5 cards for the first 15 minutes being late. After the first 15 minutes, you will receive 1 card for every minute you are late. The VCR clock is the official timekeeper.

(10)   44. No hitting, kicking, scratching, pushing, shoving, fighting, etc. If you are caught arguing and/or fighting, everyone involved will receive cards. Parents will not be detectives.

(50)   45. Any attempt to tamper with the family rules, good habit cards, daily and weekly chores lists, and/or the rewards list will result in receiving all 50 good habit cards.

A Sample List of Good Habit Cards

Good Habit Cards

1. Scrub tub and tile in downstairs bathroom.
2. Scrub tub and tile in upstairs bathroom.
3. Clean toilet in downstairs bathroom.
4. Clean toilet in upstairs bathroom.
5. Clean floor and wall in downstairs bathroom.
6. Clean floor and wall in upstairs bathroom.
7. Clean washer and dryer.
8. Clean refrigerator.
9. Dust and polish all furniture in the living room.
10. Dust and polish all furniture in the dining room.
11. Clean windows in the living room.
12. Clean windows in the dining room.
13. Clean windows in the bedrooms.
14. Clean freezer.
15. Vacuum the living room.
16. Vacuum the bedrooms.
17. Sweep and mop the kitchen floor.
18. Clean out the inside of mom's car.
19. Clean out the inside of dad's car.
20. Wash mom's car.
21. Wash dad's car.
22. Shovel/rake/sweep parking area.
23. Twenty-five pushups and twenty-five sit ups.

24. Fifty jumping jacks.
25. Remove all videos from the cabinet. Clean and dust them and put them back.
26. Shovel/rake/sweep next door neighbor's parking area.
27. Dust and clean fireplace area.
28. Clean up all the dog poop in the yard and throw away in a garbage bag.
29. Wash, dry, and put away dishes.
30. Clean microwave oven (inside and outside).
31. Clean all mirrors in the house.
32. Clear snow and ice from the walkway.
33. Dust all pictures.
34. Dust all books.
35. Write, "I will not break the rules" (100 times).
36. Do a daily chore for a sibling.
37. Clean and polish silver.
38. Clean all sinks in the house.
39. Write a two-page essay on why you shouldn't have broken the rule you just broke.
40. Remove sheets and blankets from your bed. Wash and dry them. Put them back on your bed.
41. Remove sheets and blankets from your parents bed. Wash, dry, and put back on their bed.
42. Vacuum hallway and stairs.
43. Clean laundry room floor.
44. Clean garage.
45. Write a letter to an extended family member (e.g., grandma, grandpa, aunt, uncle, cousin, etc.).
46. Bake a cake or a batch of cookies.
47. Walk the dog.
48. Give the dog a bath.
49. Dust baseboard heaters.
50. Straighten out coat/boot closet(s).

Daily Chores

1. Eat breakfast before you go to school or before you go out with friends on the weekend.
2. Make your bed in the morning before you leave for school or leave the house on the weekend.
3. Brush teeth and comb your hair in the morning before leaving for school.
4. Take a shower nightly before bedtime and use lotion on skin to keep from drying out.
5. Feed and water the dog/cat by 5:00 P.M.
6. Clean dishes immediately after dinner.

Weekly Chores

1. Clean and vacuum your bedroom by 12:00 P.M. on Saturday.
2. Take garbage cans out to the street on Thurs day evening before bed time (garbage is picked up on Friday morning).
3. Cook and have dinner ready by 5:30 P.M. on Tuesday evening.
4. Split and stack wood immediately after school on Monday. Must be done before dinner.

F A Sample List of Rewards

Tokens   **Rewards**

(2)   1. Ice-cream cone at the ice-cream parlor of your choice.

(3)   2. Video.

(25)   3. Pizza party with five friends.

(15)   4. Slumber party.

(70)   5. Nike shoes.

(12)   6. CD (must be approved by parent).

(7)   7. Roller skating.

(10   8. Hat.

(40)   9. Concert with a friend.

(15)   10. Baseball game with a friend.

(15)   11. Hockey game with a friend.

(25)   12. Dinner at your favorite restaurant.

(100)   13. Bike.

(➜)   14. Toy (8 tokens for every $10 increase in price per toy).

(200)   15. Solo trip to a relatives' home in the Lower 48.

(30)   16. Fishing trip.

(600)   17. Snow machine.

(200)   18. Your own bedroom.

(10)   19. A two-hour extension on your curfew, providing the extension is within the law.

($)   20. Money for tokens to be determined by parent(s).

G Long Term Residential Treatment

Optional Long-Term Residential Treatment Facilities/Group Homes

Child Placement Directory
Phone: 1-(530)-292-9580
E-mail: cpd@gv.net
Website: www.childplacement.com

Find a Therapist.com
Phone: 1-(800)-865-0686
E-mail: info@find-a-therapist.com
Website: www.find-a-therapist.com

Focus on the Family
A Christian based organization that provides educational resources to assist parents in raising children. They also provide referral information to assist you in contacting Christian counselors in your area. When you call them, ask for the counseling department.
Phone: 1-(800)-232-6459
Website: www.family.org

Free Resource Catalog of Treatment and Programs for Teen
Phone: 1-(800)-637-0701
Website: www.teentreatment.com

The Fold, Inc.
A Christian based group home program for boys and girls, ages 13-17. The adolescents can't have any addiction problems. Sliding fee scale available.

P.O. Box 1188
Lyndonville, VT 05851
Call for more information (e.g., brochures)
Phone: 1-(802)-626-5620
www.thefoldinc.org

(more facilities listed on next page)

Wilderness Therapy and Treatment
E-mail: info@wilderness-threapy.org
Website: www.wilderness-therapy.org

Willow Springs Center
(A residential treatment center for children and adolescents. You can use your insurance with this treatment facility)

690 Edison Way
Reno, Nevada 89502
Call for more information (e.g., brochures and a video tape)
Phone: 1-(800)-448-9454

World Wide Association of Specialty Programs/Teen Help
(Most likely the best long-term residential treatment programs on the planet)

These facilities provide long-term residential treatment for girls and boys (ages 12-18). They have facilities located in Montana (boys and girls), Utah (boys and girls), South Carolina (boys and girls), Jamaica (boys and girls), and Mexico (boys and girls). Call Teen Help for more information (e.g., brochures and video tapes). Ask them to mail you the application/admission packet. Also, ask for the student loan information. These facilities are college prep/long-term residential treatment facilities. Most insurance companies will not reimburse for services provided via Teen Help.

Phone: 1-(800)-355-8336   www.schoolsforteens.com

Yellowstone Boys and Girls Ranch
A Christian based residential/group home program for boys, ages 6-18, and girls, ages 12-18. Treatment covered by insurance. This program rivals Teen Help

1732 S. 72nd St. W
Billings, MT 59106-3599
Phone: 1-(800)-726-6755   www.ybgr.org

Note:
If your are aware of a high quality long term residential treatment facility and/or group home for children and adolescents, please contact Dr. Matthew A. Johnson and let him know about it so he can consider placing the information in the next edition of *FAMILY Rules: Positive Parenting with a Plan (Grades K-12)*.

H   *Professional Escorts*

Escorts are needed sometimes to help transport a child to a treatment facility if they are unwilling to cooperate. You can lead a horse to water and make it drink even if it doesn't want to! Escorts work!

Call: Ann Atwood at "Teen Escorts"
1-(800)-322-3094

or

Call: Dr. Matthew A. Johnson
1-(541)-956-8585
e-mail: drj@family-rules.com
Website: www.family-rules.com

I   *How to Schedule a FAMILY Rules Seminar*

If you like what you read and would like to schedule a FAMILY Rules seminar at your business, school, church, synagogue, or civic organization so other families in your community can benefit, please contact Dr. Matthew A. Johnson via the following options:

Telephone Number: 1-(541)-956-8585

E-mail Address: drj@family-rules.com

Fax Number: 1-(541)-955-7165

Yes! Dr. Matthew A. Johnson does live in Grants Pass, Oregon and it may seem far, far away from where you live. Yes! I know you can't ever imagine traveling that far yourself. However, due to the modern miracle of avionics, Dr. Matthew A. Johnson is actually able to fly to your location via a jet airplane. The neighboring city of Medford, Oregon really does have an international airport and Dr. Matthew A. Johnson can get to your community in a jiffy. Amazing, huh? So don't hesitate to contact him to schedule a FAMILY Rules seminar in your community. He really wouldn't mind traveling to your neck of the woods to present his FAMILY Rules seminar to the families in your community. Besides, where you live is probably a very nice place to visit. "Dr. J." could use an occasional change of scenery from time to time.

J *Matthew A. Johnson*

Dr. Matthew Johnson:
Licensed Clinical Phychologist

Counseling Provided for Children, Adolescents, and Adults to address the following issues:

Attention Deficit Disorder (ADD)
Defiant Behaviors in Children and Adolescents (Behavior Modification)
Depression, including Seasonal Affective Disorder (SAD)
Generalized Anxiety, including Panic Attacks and Phobias
Sexual Abuse and Sex Addiction
Grief and Loss
Alcohol and Drug Abuse Assessment and Counseling
Dysfunctional Family issues (ACOA's, Codependency)
Individual, Couples, and Family Counseling

Psychological Testing Services Provided to Children, Adolescents, and Adults to Assess for:

Objective Computerized Assessment of Attention Deficit Disorder (ADD)
Intellectual Deficits (IQ Testing)
Academic Achievement
Personality Strengths and Weaknesses
Depression and/or Anxiety
Screening for Neuropsychological Impairment
Alcohol and Drug Abuse

Appointments Available in Grants Pass, Oregon 1-(541)-955-7132
Counseling and Testing Services Reimbursed by Most Insurance Companies

Grants Pass, Oregon Office:
PO Box 1801
Grants Pass, Oregon 97528
Wk: 1-(541)-955-7132
Fax: 1-(541)-955-7165
e-mail address: drj@family-rules.com
Website: www.family-rules.com